Tossed to the Wind

TOSSED TO THE WIND

Stories of Hurricane Maria Survivors

María T. Padilla and Nancy Rosado

UNIVERSITY OF FLORIDA PRESS

GAINESVILLE

25 24 23 22 21 20   6 5 4 3 2 1

Library of Congress Control Number: 2019950422
ISBN 978-1-68340-150-6

University of Florida Press
2046 NE Waldo Road
Suite 2100
Gainesville, FL 32609
http://upress.ufl.edu

UF PRESS

UNIVERSITY
OF FLORIDA

To my mom, Genoveva Colberg;

husband, Keith Constantine;

and daughter, Sarahí Constantine-Padilla

—the partners in my life who listen to all my stories.

To Herminia Flores Rodríguez, *mi querida madre*,

who taught me to love Puerto Rico and my culture;

to my partner, Myrna Villalobos, who supports my every endeavor;

and to my Puerto Rican community, whose resilience never ceases

to amaze me.

CONTENTS

PREFACE

Flying to Puerto Rico on October 20, 2017, the first thing that caught my eye was the harsh contrast of the cerulean-blue tarps covering so many homes in San Juan and its surrounding area versus the grayish brown of . . . everything. It was one month to the day that Hurricane Maria had devastated the island and destroyed its power grid, leaving more than 3 million people in the dark. In the moments just before landing, there came the immediate realization that what I and the other passengers on the flight had brought to help our compatriots and families would have little to no real impact. It would not be enough, I perceived as my eyes filled with tears. The magnitude of the devastation that Maria caused as it ripped through Puerto Rico was incalculable a month later, a year later, and even to this day in mental and emotional terms.

The sense of hopelessness was palpable but never more so than after nightfall, when the dark-blue sky illuminated nothing, and there was little left to do but wait for sleep. It was in the stillness of the dark, after batteries had given out and candles had melted into wax sculptures, that people faced the loss of control over their lives. The daylight had tricked everyone into thinking that in some way, however small, they still held the reins. But it was not true. It was in the night that Puerto Ricans rediscovered that their force of will had been overpowered by the forces of nature.

Relief efforts focused on the basic requirements of food, water, and shelter. The priority of fulfilling these needs seemed to preempt another need that only now is beginning to be addressed: mental health services. And with good reason. All things tangible became a primary focus while the seemingly diaphanous was placed on hold. Nonetheless, in the aftermath of disaster we instinctively tend to repeat our experiences out loud to family and friends, trying to merge and make sense of our memories, physical experiences, and emotional states. It is a way of making sense out of the senseless. Just as important, storytelling also allows us to control and manage the chaos, if only in our minds, that comes in the wake of disaster.

Having arrived in Puerto Rico with supplies to distribute as part of a relief project called Adopta un pueblo, my coworkers and I had the opportunity to interact with communities across the island. Our experience from town to town was quite consistent. We would deliver supplies to an individual or family, and they would, with no prompting, gift us with amazing stories of survival, loss, and hope for recovery or a new beginning in the States. My coworkers and I learned that to pause and listen in the midst of handing out supplies was as valuable and important as distributing the supplies we had brought. The small gift of time from total strangers allowed for validation and the processing of feelings and emotions that might otherwise have remained an internal conversation. These stories had a profound impact on us. Inevitably, as evening fell and daylight gave way to darkness, we discussed what we had heard as the unpleasant odor of the diesel that powered home generators filled the air around us.

Mission completed, we returned to central Florida only to find the entire state preparing for the influx of Puerto Ricans fleeing the island. While I busied myself with raising funds to purchase solar light bulbs to send to communities in Puerto Rico to help combat the depression that seemed to come with nightfall, welcome centers had opened at major airports to provide thousands of Maria survivors with immediate services such as filing FEMA (Federal Emergency Management Agency) claims, searching for housing, and obtaining driver's licenses. Chaotic at times but still functional, the welcome centers offered evacuees a sense of order, hope, and normalcy—a far cry from the frustration and disorganization they experienced on the island.

In assessing the needs of the evacuees, the intake workers of various agencies at the airports became the first to hear their stories of despair, survival, and hope. There is bravery in leaving all that you have and know to start over as a stranger in a strange land. Under more normal circumstances, the excitement of a new beginning and new possibilities is balanced by the deliberate planning for contingencies to generate a successful outcome. But these were not normal circumstances. For the many who made the decision to leave Puerto Rico after Hurricane Maria, their bravery was overshadowed by a question of survival.

Their homes and cars had been destroyed, schools and hospitals closed, and jobs lost, and the uncertainty of obtaining food and water on a consistent basis forced the realization that life on the island as they had known it would never be the same. Thus, it was not a question of choice but of how and when to leave for those whose children suffered from serious illnesses or had special needs; for seniors who had lost their homes along with a lifetime of possessions; and for anyone who felt the fatigue and uncertainty of trying to rebuild their lives amid utter chaos.

Upon arriving in Orlando, I felt the weight of the narratives I had been privileged to listen to in Puerto Rico. I became aware of a different type of narrative, a continuing narrative, of the evacuees who had journeyed to central Florida, focused more on adjustment and overcoming obstacles, while feeling resentment at having been driven from their homes, the life they knew, and the country they loved. I am convinced that these stories are part of the long Puerto Rican experience in the United States and are worthy of being documented lest they be forgotten or distorted by time.

With this in mind, I contacted my friend María Padilla, a former reporter for the *Orlando Sentinel* and editor of two Orlando-area Spanish-language newspapers, and suggested we collect the oral histories of those who had left Puerto Rico after Hurricane Maria in an effort to document the continuing Puerto Rican migration to central Florida. We shopped the idea around until, fortuitously, a mutual academic friend, Patricia Silver, an expert on central Florida's Puerto Rican diaspora, pointed us in the direction of the University of Florida Press, which enthusiastically embraced our ideas. *Tossed to the Wind: Stories of Hurricane Maria Survivors* is the result of our efforts.

Nancy Rosado, MSW

1

A STORM FOR THE AGES

María T. Padilla

On the night of September 20, 2017, Coralis Alméstica Cintrón and her seventy-six-year-old grandmother hid from the Category 4 fury of Hurricane Maria in their Sierra Bayamón home outside of San Juan, Puerto Rico. When the storm blew the aluminum awning off their outdoor terrace, it was clear that Maria had found them. The two clung to each other during the terror of Maria, as they have throughout most of their lives. Two weeks earlier, twenty-year-old Coralis and her *abuela* had endured Hurricane Irma, which left them without water and electricity for about a week. Irma had not delivered the storm that meteorologists promised, bypassing the island and lulling many Puerto Ricans into a false sense of security.[1] As another hurricane neared, Coralis and her grandmother hadn't done enough to prepare for Maria.

Coralis gathered water in plastic jugs and collected ice, but those preparations were not sufficient, given the wrath and destruction that Maria would wreak on the island. The second hurricane in as many weeks plunged Coralis, her *abuela*, and all of Puerto Rico's 3.3 million people into total darkness, a blackness that lasted not for a night or two but for months, making it the worst blackout in American history and the second-worst in the history of the world.[2] After the hurricane, Coralis and her neighbors went house to house on their Sierra Bayamón street, checking on families, sharing, bartering, and exchanging what they could, always scurrying to return home before night blanketed the island. But the tap water was undrinkable, roads were nearly impassable, food was scarce, and lines were long at banks, supermarkets, and gas stations. A university student, Coralis couldn't attend classes because all schools were closed. Her already thin frame was now twenty pounds lighter. Coralis sensed that life in Puerto Rico had become a lot more difficult and would never be the same. Everything seemed to have collapsed around her. She had to do something. Just two weeks after Hurricane Maria struck Puerto Rico, Coralis made the tough decision to pack her bags and hurry off the island, leaving her *abuela* behind. She soon would be joined by tens of thousands of others fleeing on flights to Florida and other states for similar reasons: they had no idea or sense of when life in Puerto Rico would return to normal. It would become a Puerto Rican migration of unprecedented, modern-day proportions, with the potential to deplete the island of young, vibrant, working talent while also boosting the more than 5.4 million Puerto Ricans already living in the States, about 2 million more than on the island. Before the hurricane hit, Florida alone was home to more than 1 million Puerto Ricans. More would soon arrive.

Hurricane Maria was a 1-in-3,000 event that trapped people in their homes and communities and caused damages totaling billions of dollars to buildings, highways, water supplies, and the electric grid.[3] It frightened adults and children alike with a growl so primal and primitive that people ran for safety to bedrooms, bathrooms, closets, and hallways—anything to get away from the terrifying noise as the "palm and banana trees began that long distance talk with rain."[4] People like Coralis watched stunned as Category 4 winds of over 155 miles per hour tore off roofs and street signs; smashed windows, awnings, and cars; snapped trees; and crashed electrical lines and lamp posts to the ground. Residents tried mopping up leaks with towels and threw out buckets of water to prevent further damage to hearth and home. As the water rose to dangerous levels, still others fled their homes in the midst of the hurricane, seeking higher ground or refuge with neighbors.

Hurricane Maria entered Puerto Rico through the town of Yabucoa, on the southeastern coast, as the eighth hurricane of the 2017 Atlantic hurricane season. Maria had gathered strength over several days, becoming an extremely dan-

View of the interior of a home in Loíza.

Bare pine trees and debris left by Hurricane Maria on Luquillo Beach.

A homeowner in Cataño assesses damage to his roof.

Roof stripped off of a home in Loíza where a street lamp snapped from its wood post and is lying across a chain-link fence.

Car driving under fallen lamp posts in Loíza.

Hurricane-ravaged meeting hall of the Fishermen's Association, Crash Boat Beach, Aguadilla.

Home destroyed by Hurricane Maria in town of Isabela. The tent behind the home was being used by the homeowner as temporary shelter.

gerous Category 5 storm in a period of eighteen hours between September 17 and 19, 2017. By the time it made landfall in Yabucoa, Maria had already ravaged the small Windward Island of Dominica with sustained winds of more than 175 miles per hour. It remained a Category 5 as it swooshed across the Caribbean, losing slight steam and downgrading into a high-end Category 4 hurricane with winds of over 155 miles per hour as it approached the US Virgin Island of St. Croix and the Puerto Rico archipelago. Maria moved in a west-northwesterly direction over the island, crashing into the interior mountain zone and northwestern portions of the island, and exiting through Quebradillas. Hurricane-force winds spread from corner to corner in Puerto Rico, accompanied by extremely heavy rainfall that produced major to catastrophic flooding and flash flooding. Even as the storm eased offshore, tropical storm–force winds continued to lash the island into the evening of September 21 and the morning of September 22.[5] When Maria was finished, it was painfully clear that the hurricane had wreaked ruin and generated a vast amount of rubble on the island, a United States territory for 121 years with 3.3 million people.[6] Maria defoliated the verdant hills and mountains of the enchanted emerald island, leaving behind an unrecognizable muddy, burned-out landscape with stumps for trees as far as the eye could see. It seemed that Maria left nothing untouched or undamaged, to wit:

- Nearly thirty inches of rain, possibly more, were deposited in forty-eight hours in the central mountain zone. Drier spots received six to eight inches of rain.
- Up to twenty-five landslides per square kilometer occurred across the entire midsection of Puerto Rico, with the mountain town of Utuado receiving the brunt: more than twenty-five landslides per square kilometer.
- Rivers crested as much as thirty-seven feet above stage height in the case of the Río Grande de Manatí in the northwest town of Manatí to fourteen feet above stage height for the Río Portugués near the southern town of Ponce.
- Two tornadoes touched down near the Yabucoa post office, and a third tornado was observed east of Highway 3 and north of Highway 901, also near Yabucoa.[7]

Worst of all, from one thousand to five thousand lives may have been lost due to the disaster or its horrible aftermath, as Puerto Ricans went without essen-

Downed power lines in town of Rincón.

Home in Rincón almost swept into the ocean.

Above: Solid cement guest house in Rincón destroyed by Hurricane Maria.

Left: Car crushed by second floor of a home in Rincón.

Signage stripped from its framing in Aguadilla.

tial services, including access to medical care. Puerto Rico governor Ricardo Rosselló and the Trump administration cast doubt on the reported death toll in an ugly, months-long national dispute that played out in blaring news head-lines. No doubt this took an additional emotional toll on an already burdened population. The catastrophe had its beginning long before the hurricane hit, but, as in a classic play, its denouement was brought on by Maria. This is how the Hurricane Maria tragedy played out in twelve acts.

A community improvised a bridge in Adjuntas.

Cleaning up in the aftermath of Hurricane Maria in La Perla, San Juan.

Above: Hurricane-damaged roofs in La Perla, San Juan.

Left: A centennial tree leans across a street and rests on the roof of an Old San Juan colonial home.

Two uprooted palm trees seem to embrace a home in Piñones outside of San Juan.

No Modern Memory

Puerto Ricans had no modern memory or experience of a catastrophic hurricane like Maria. The last hurricane of similar or worse magnitude to devastate Puerto Rico occurred nearly one hundred years earlier: San Felipe II, a 1928 Category 4 hurricane that scored a direct hit with sustained winds of 144 miles per hour and hurricane-force winds that lasted more than eighteen hours. Felipe II caused a staggering $50 million in property damage, equal to more than $743 million today based on US inflation-adjusted dollars, leaving hundreds of thousands of residents without homes. Miraculously, however, Felipe II killed only about three hundred people in Puerto Rico, in sharp contrast with what followed days later, when the same storm swamped Lake Okeechobee, Florida, claiming nearly three thousand lives and generating $100 million in damages, equivalent to $1.48 billion today in US inflation-adjusted dollars.[8] Before Felipe II, Hurricane San Ciriaco had snuffed out more than three thousand lives in Puerto Rico in 1899,[9] just a year after the United States military marched into Puerto Rico, claiming the island as its territory after the Cuban-Spanish-American War. Hurricane Maria's northwesterly path was eerily similar to that of San Ciriaco, named after a Catholic patron feast day, as most hurricanes were at the time.

Life after Maria immediately became unbearably difficult, even dangerous, for the majority of Puerto Ricans. Maria isolated families and friends after 95 percent of cellular towers collapsed. Many took to the highways in search of a cellular signal, creating a common sight throughout the island of huddled masses trying to pick up radio waves by roadside cell towers. One hundred percent of Puerto Rico Aqueduct and Sewer Authority customers lost drinking water, forcing people to search for sources of water flowing down mountainsides and through pipes placed there many years earlier. The toppling of the island's already crumbling electric grid meant that 100 percent of electric customers lost power. Some customers didn't get power turned back on for as long as eleven months after the storm.[10] Approximately 3.93 billion hours of electrical service were lost, more than in the rest of the United States over a five-year period from a combination of sources. It may well be the second-largest blackout in the world, behind Typhoon Haiyan in the Philippines in 2013.[11] The lack of basic services caused many people to suffer extreme deprivation and loss, as people also went without food, which became scarce. About 85 percent of Puerto Rico's food is imported, mostly from the States,[12] but the ports were closed for nearly a week, and food couldn't be distributed. Even if that had been possible, there was no electricity (refrigeration) to keep food from rotting. People resorted to old-fashioned ways of cooking, using *leña* (firewood) and charcoal, as their grandmothers and great-grandmothers had once prepared meals. The search for food, water, gasoline, and cash became a daily stressor and ordeal for the vast majority of the population, adding to the emotional and physical toll of the disaster. Lines at gas stations, supermarkets, and ATMs began forming in the wee hours each morning, and people had no clue as to whether supplies would run out before they reached the head of the line. The lack of essential services is believed to be a major factor in the loss of thousands of lives in Puerto Rico.

Over 90 percent of hospitals were impacted, and many doctors' offices and pharmacies were shut down for days after the hurricane, leaving the elderly, sick, and infirm—an increasing proportion of the island's population[13]—

A tire rim is converted into a stove for cooking at a home in the mountain town of Adjuntas.

forced to forgo necessary medication and healthcare. Many patients dependent on treatments requiring electricity—from dialysis and respirators to nebulizers—were forced to do without. The government of Puerto Rico pegged the official number of deaths at a low sixty-four, causing an outcry from people who had lived a different experience and had heard anecdotal reports of deaths from family, friends, and neighbors. The Center for Investigative Journalism in Puerto Rico was the first to report, in September 2017, that the number of deaths related to Hurricane Maria was being underreported. The center later estimated that 985 more people died after the storm, mainly the elderly in hospitals and group homes, compared with the same period in 2016.[14] In May 2018, the *New England Journal of Medicine* published a study by the Harvard University T. H. Chan School of Public Health (and others) stating that Maria-related deaths could be over 4,600.[15] Later, Governor Rosselló hired the Milken Institute for Public Health at George Washington University to audit the island's hurricane deaths and settle the score. The Milken Institute concluded that there were 2,975 hurricane-related deaths, dealing a mighty blow to the credibility of the government's long-held estimate of sixty-four. The Milken study blamed the inaccuracy of the official fatality figure on a lack of death-certification protocols by medical professionals, among other things.[16] However, even before the Milken Institute study was published in August 2018, the Rosselló administration had quietly updated its estimate of hurricane deaths to 1,427 in a report to Congress dated July 2018.[17]

An Island under Water

Hurricane Maria's extensive damage to infrastructure, homes, workplaces, and the Puerto Rican psyche was exacerbated by Puerto Rico's ongoing economic debacle, closely linked to the often fraught and disjointed one-hundred-plus-year relationship with its United States overlord, always a sore spot for Puerto Ricans. The dysfunctional interaction created a recovery of fits and starts. Puerto Ricans rightly worried whether the United States, meaning Congress and the federal government apparatus, would be fair in its treatment of Puerto Rico in the face of the calamitous event, given the existing inequitable political and financial handling of the island. Who would advocate for Puerto Rico, its people, and its recovery if it had only one nonvoting member of Congress compared with the two senators and dozens of congressional representatives for most other states? Would Puerto Rico get a fair share of help given existing imbalances in certain federal programs?[18] Did Americans in the States understand that Puerto Ricans are citizens? A Morning Consult poll conducted immediately after Maria showed that only 54 percent of American adults understood that Puerto Ricans are also American citizens.

Plus, the federal government's inept response to Maria, as indicated later in this chapter, provided fresh fodder for the narrative of the island's pro-statehood faction, which portrays Puerto Rico as second-class with a nebulous political status as neither self-governing nor a state. Every federal misstep, and there were many, became entangled with Governor Rosselló and his New Progressive Party's push for Puerto Rico statehood, seen as a way to provide equality for Puerto Ricans. Historically, each New Progressive Party administration pushes hard for statehood, and Rosselló's was no different, conducting a political status plebiscite in June 2017 in which 97 percent voted for statehood but in which less than a quarter of the voting-age population cast a ballot, undermining the result. It was one in a long series of nonbinding status plebiscites, meaning Congress did not have to adhere to the results, putting off for yet another day the question of Puerto Rico's political limbo.[19]

121 Years of Uncertainty

Puerto Ricans had every right to be suspicious of the federal government's reaction and role in the hurricane response because the island has been treated as second-class for 121 years—not just in American attitudes but, more important, in American law. In 1901, just three years after the United States claimed Puerto Rico as its own, a series of cases rose to the US Supreme Court that to this day define Puerto Rico's relationship to the United States: namely that Puerto Rico and several other territories such as Guam and the US Virgin Islands are *subordinate* to the rest of the nation, going against the grain of the equality clause of the US Constitution.[20] The Supreme Court cases, about twenty-one in all and known as the Insular Cases, remain fairly obscure in the United States' civil rights canon but resonate today in significant and surprising ways.

According to one case, *Downes v. Bidwell* (1901), often considered the most important Insular Case, Puerto Rico was determined to be "foreign to the United States in a domestic sense," an incoherent legal argument that nonetheless paved the way for Puerto Rico to be treated differently from the states. According to this thinking, because Puerto Rico was not legally incorporated into the United States, as other territories had been—Hawaii and Alaska were incorporated in 1903 and 1905, respectively—the island remained *outside* the nation, and therefore the US Constitution didn't apply to it. Since the Constitution didn't apply to Puerto Rico, that left Congress with sole power over the island, a situation that continues to this day. Puerto Rico is represented in Congress by exactly one nonvoting delegate and no US senators despite its population of over 3 million people. Congress made this determination in the Foraker Act of 1900, significantly curtailing Puerto Rico's ability to influence Congress. All federal laws and federal policies apply to Puerto Rico in real terms every day, but the island has little to no input in the creation of such laws and policies and instead must go begging for friends in Congress—that is, representatives with full congressional voting power—to raise the volume of its political voice. Even when Congress extended US citizenship to Puerto Ricans in 1917 under the Jones Act, a US Supreme Court Insular Case, *Balzac v. Puerto Rico* (1922), later reiterated that although Puerto Ricans were granted citizenship, "It doesn't make Puerto Ricans part of the United States."[21]

That opinion was later underscored in the 1989–91 congressional hearings into Puerto Rico's political status when the Congressional Research Service concluded in a letter to the Senate Energy Resources Committee that oversees Puerto Rico affairs that since Puerto Rico wasn't really a part of the United States, it must also be true that persons born in Puerto Rico do not possess birthright citizenship under the Fourteenth Amendment. The letter further stated that if Congress so chose, it could take away the citizenship it granted earlier to Puerto Ricans.[22] Scholars have disputed the argument, noting that Puerto Rico was defined as part of the United States in the Nationality Act of 1940, which indicated that a birth in Puerto Rico is tantamount to a birth in the United States for purposes of birthright citizenship.[23]

The US Supreme Court that ruled against Puerto Rico in so many Insular Cases, setting the lopsided tone for United States–Puerto Rico relations for decades to come, is the same court, plus or minus a few members, that ruled against African Americans in *Plessy v. Ferguson* (1896), a decision that resulted in the "separate but equal" doctrine that relegated African Americans to second-class citizenship—even after slavery was officially ended under the Thirteenth Amendment to the Constitution (1865), even after all persons born or naturalized in the United States including former slaves were granted birthright citizenship with equal rights under the law under the Fourteenth Amendment (1868), and even after states were prohibited from disenfranchising voters based on race, color, or previous servitude under the Fifteenth Amendment (1870).[24] In effect, Puerto Ricans were made—in a phrase taken from the US Supreme Court decision *Plessy v. Ferguson*—"separate but equal" soon after the United States' takeover of Puerto Rico through a stream of US Supreme Court decisions codifying racial and ethnic bias and, in the case of the territories, creating an American colonial empire in which territorial residents had little recourse. In the eyes of scholars, the United States has created political ghettoes in the territories from which residents cannot escape, for which there is no correction, creating a "political apartheid" for US citizens in Puerto Rico and other territories.[25] *Plessy* was overturned by the decision in the *Brown v. Board of Education* (1954) school desegregation case, but there has been no equivalent case for Puerto Rico. Puerto Ricans continue to live under the yoke of the Insular Case rulings that brand Puerto Rico as separate and decidedly unequal, a philosophy resulting in disparate treatment in national programs, especially regarding funding, a major concern of the Puerto Rico government, particularly in the face of Hurricane Maria recovery. In programs such as Supplemental Security Income (SSI) and Medicaid, among others, funding for Puerto Rico follows a different formula from that used in the fifty states.

The legacy of the Insular Cases continues to resonate in peculiar ways, for instance in one of the most searing legal and political battles of the 2000s: concerning the rights of enemy combatants detained in the US Guantánamo Bay prison in Cuba. The Bush administration argued that the detainees had no rights because Guantánamo was outside of the United States, a legal maneuver harking back to the Insular Cases.[26] The US Supreme Court disagreed, stating that the detainees were entitled to limited rights and protections such as habeas corpus. But make no mistake, the Bush administration drew a direct line between the highly discriminatory Insular Cases of the early twentieth century and a twenty-first-century issue, proving that if one set of people can be devalued, others can be, too.

A Foggy Economic Scenario

Puerto Rico's fuzzy political status was complicated by an equally foggy economic scenario, as Puerto Rico was reeling from a more than ten-year recession when Hurricane Maria struck the island. Annual payments on more than $70 billion in long-term debt had crippled the island's economy and sent hundreds of thousands of migrants fleeing to the States, most notably Florida, in search of employment and a better quality of life. Puerto Rico's financial collapse began in 2006 and was attributed to Congress's elimination of a federal tax incentive that successfully lured companies and jobs to Puerto Rico. While Puerto Ricans were still coping with the loss of the federal tax credit, the financial collapse and economic recession hit the island, generating economic contractions in each fiscal year except fiscal year 2012. The worst years, 2009 and 2010, produced about an annual 4 percent decline.

Puerto Rico increasingly offered up a panorama of shrinking opportunities as companies and government slashed jobs. By 2013, barely 40 percent of the labor force was working.[27] The financial crisis came to a head when government coffers began to run dry as debt payments soaked up more of the island's operating income, affecting the government's ability to fund itself. In a vicious cycle, Puerto Rico's response was to borrow still more money to finance its deficits in what became an excessive reliance on public financing. There was little money to invest in public infrastructure, accounting for the crumbling state of the island's electric grid and water supply, among other things, when Maria slammed into the island. From fiscal year 2001 onward, Puerto Rico's public debt grew steadily, surpassing its economic output or gross national product in 2013.[28] Former governor Alejandro García Padilla finally sounded the public alarm, declaring in 2015 that Puerto Rico's more than $73 billion in debt was actually more when pensions and other liabilities were included and that it was "not payable." Puerto Rico later attempted to declare bankruptcy but could not because, in another political and economic inequity, it doesn't fall under federal municipal bankruptcy laws.[29] Instead, Congress in 2016 passed the Puerto Rico Oversight, Management, and Economic Stability Act, or PROMESA, staving off creditors from suing the island and placing Puerto Rico in a form of receivership. The move came with a high political cost as critics argued that the appointed fiscal control board breached the sovereignty of the supposed self-governing territory. In May 2017, just weeks before the official start of the hurricane season, the oversight board declared a certain type of bankruptcy, stating presciently that the island government couldn't provide its citizens with effective services.[30]

Cascading Failures

That's where Puerto Rico stood when Hurricane Maria showed up cruising to bruise in September 2017. The island was in no fiscal or administrative shape to handle a catastrophe of such magnitude, as events later proved. Which means that people gave nature too much credit for the disaster, for the hurricane was both a horrendous natural phenomenon as well as a man-made one. A series of cascading failures on the part of local and federal governments created a humanitarian crisis in Puerto Rico. "Natural disasters are never natural. They are always the result of what people and governments do before and after the event," wrote historian Stuart B. Schwartz about the effects of disasters on political systems.[31] Just as Puerto Rico's handling of its finances was messy and to the detriment of the island's economic well-being, so, too, was Puerto Rico's management of its personnel bureaucracy, the first line of defense in a natural disaster. The island has long been known for running a bloated ship—and even after belt tightening, Puerto Rico's central and municipal governments employed 24 percent of the workforce, or one of every four workers in fiscal year 2017.[32] Worse, many government workers are considered political hires, including as many as 50 percent of employees at the Puerto Rico Electric Power Authority (PREPA), the keepers of the island's outdated, faulty, and failing electric grid.[33] Across the bureaucracy, no employees were trained to handle a Category 4 hurricane like Maria. There was no expertise in emergency or crisis communication and planning among varying agencies on an island strategically situated along the Caribbean's hurricane alley. Existing plans, such as they were, were not updated or coordinated among agencies, leading to "an inoperable and disconnected" emergency response, one lacking clarity about crisis and emergency risk protocols.[34] It didn't help that Governor Rosselló was in the first year of his administration and had never before held elected office. No one knew what to do, aggravating the life-and-death situations Puerto Ricans faced. Even PREPA's month-long delay in seeking immediate mutual aid from stateside utilities—a common practice during natural disasters—prolonged power outages, severely impacting island residents and contributing to the rising death toll. Residents complained of the lack of municipal response, despite an army of fifty-eight thousand workers in seventy-eight island towns. Many residents said they never heard from their municipalities, the most local form of government and one that presumably knows and understands its area and population best. It turns out that communication between municipal and central government was "inefficient and ineffective for catastrophic disasters." Astonishingly, the municipal affairs unit of the governor's office didn't interact with municipalities for emergency communications. It's no wonder that about 40 percent of municipalities experienced significant mortality increases.[35]

The "who's-on-first, what's-on-second, and I-don't-know-is-on-third" central and municipal government responses to Hurricane Maria resulted not only from a lack of training but also from a lack of financial resources to stockpile supplies and even provide space for warehousing. That complicated federal government efforts, which, by the time Maria barreled through Puerto Rico, were already tasked with handling disasters in Texas after Hurricane Harvey and Florida's Hurricane Irma. Still to come were the California wildfires, further straining existing resources. Puerto Rico's lack of preparedness forced the Federal Emergency Management Agency (FEMA) to take on a first-responder role, a function usually reserved for local governments. FEMA, in turn, requested that other departments, such as the Department of Defense and the Army Corps of Engineers, also assume first-responder responsibilities, such as installing electric generators and tarps and removing hurricane debris.[36] Add Puerto Rico's thousand-mile distance from Florida, the nearest state, its crumbling infrastructure, its bloated but untrained bureaucracy, and its rugged and, after the hurricane, impassable mountainous terrain, and the dominoes fell into place for an extremely challenging hurricane recovery effort.

A Complicated Response

FEMA's major deficiencies complicated recovery efforts as well, and it later acknowledged that some of its staff was not able to withstand Puerto Rico's posthurricane "extreme or austere environment."[37] The agency didn't have enough disaster-certified personnel to handle the response, creating a potential negative impact on services, nor did it have enough bilingual employees to communicate effectively with the residents of the Spanish-speaking territory. The number of FEMA staff deployed to Puerto Rico was 2,805 in November 2017, or two months after the storm, far below the Texas peak of 5,964 two months after Harvey in October 2017, despite the greater catastrophic need in Puerto Rico.[38] Because the infrastructure collapse isolated Puerto Rico's population, FEMA was required to be more hands-on, conducting more door-to-door visits to assess damages and needs and provide individual assistance. However, the hurricane had destroyed the ease of traveling, and finding addresses, always difficult in Puerto Rico, became more difficult.[39] What's more, FEMA didn't heed a disaster-preparedness exercise and report dated 2011 that revealed that Puerto Rico would require "extensive support" to move and distribute commodities on the island.[40]

In fact, a University of Michigan study later found that the federal government responded unequally to Maria, with faster reaction, more staff, and more money for Hurricanes Harvey in Texas and Irma in Florida, compared with Maria, even though Harvey and Irma caused less damage relative to Maria in Puerto Rico. The study notes, "Assuming that disaster responses should be commensurate to the degree of storm severity and need of the population, the federal response is questionable and the degree of variation between the disaster responses is problematic."[41] The Michigan researchers found that Harvey and Irma survivors received $100 million in federal recovery aid within nine days of the disasters, compared with $6 million for Puerto Rico in an equal period of time. The disparate treatment of Puerto Rico may bear long-term consequences, especially in survivors' health outcomes: "Disaster responses that differ substantially for reasons other than storm severity and needs of the affected area may affect the public health as well as the health equity of the individuals and communities living through the disaster and the recovery."[42]

More than 1.1 million people in Puerto Rico applied for FEMA disaster-related housing assistance after Irma and Maria, but only 3.5 percent received help.[43] That includes 33,016 who benefited from interim repairs allowing people to stay in their homes and 6,907 with hotel vouchers or Transitional Sheltering Assistance (TSA), which the government of Puerto Rico didn't request until over a month after the hurricane.[44] The average wait time for inspections of damaged or destroyed properties was thirty-nine days in Puerto Rico, longer than for states affected by other hurricanes, including Katrina in Louisiana. In addition, two months after the hurricane struck fewer inspections had taken place—261,000 versus 1.4 million for Katrina and 967,000 for Irma. The figure was revised in May 2018 to more than 803,000.[45]

The United States' long-conflicted attitude toward disaster relief in general—that is, whether disaster aid promotes dependency or whether people should be self-sustaining—intruded into the recovery effort. The initial colonial encounter between the United States and Puerto Rico at the turn of the twentieth century established a narrative that today would be considered racist: that Puerto Ricans are lazy and therefore undeserving of aid. An early American anthropologist in Puerto Rico described the people as "having rather unintelligent faces," primitive, illiterate, idolatrous, destitute, superstitious, and dark-skinned, paving the way for Puerto Ricans to be considered as "Other" and justifying American rule over "natives."[46] After Hurricane San

Ciriaco of 1899, Congress did not approve disaster-relief funds for Puerto Rico, a strange reaction to the Category 4 storm that leveled the island. Months later Congress outlawed the Puerto Rican peso in a move that further impoverished the island.[47] Later, for Hurricane San Felipe II in 1928, aid to Puerto Rico came in the form of charitable donations and interest-bearing loans.[48] The condescending attitude came to a head when President Donald Trump, in advance of a visit to Puerto Rico in October 2017, declared in a tweet, "They want everything to be done for them when it should be a community effort."[49] Trump's visit to Puerto Rico produced the now infamous photo of the president throwing rolls of paper towels to a cheering crowd at a chapel in the affluent town of Guaynabo near San Juan. During his visit he complained that the cost of recovery would "throw the federal budget out of whack."[50] As the first-year anniversary of Maria approached in 2018, the president caused an uproar when he tweeted that he didn't believe that thousands had died due to the storm, blaming the "inflated numbers" on partisan politics.[51] And later, in early 2019, Trump was still venting in tweet mode, stating that Puerto Rico's elected officials were "grossly incompetent" and adding that "Puerto Rico got far more money than Texas & Florida combined, yet their government can't do anything right, the place is a mess—nothing works." He incorrectly asserted that Puerto Rico had received $91 billion in aid, far more than Texas and Florida, when the actual figure was nearly ten times less, or $11 billion.[52]

The federal government's disparate response to Maria shone a harsh spotlight on the disenfranchisement of Puerto Rico, and, naturally, Puerto Rico's pro-statehood New Progressive Party pounced. In June 2018, while the island was still in the midst of basic recovery (all Puerto Ricans wouldn't have electricity again until August 2018), Puerto Rico resident commissioner Jenniffer González filed a bill to make the island the fifty-first state by 2021. At a Washington, D.C., news conference, Governor Rosselló declared: "No longer do we want ambiguity. No longer do we want this kicked down the road. In Congress you're either with us or against the people of Puerto Rico."[53] That bill went nowhere, as happens with many bills addressing Puerto Rico's political status. In early 2019 Rosselló was back, this time with Florida congressman Darren Soto (D-9), Arizona representative Rubén Gallego (D-7), and Delegate González in tow as cosponsors of a new statehood bill influenced in large measure by the substandard federal disaster-recovery response in Puerto Rico. However, the bill also generated immediate criticism as a unilateral move that lacked con-sultation with Puerto Rico voters.[54] Predictably, the bill went nowhere.

Despite glaring inefficiencies and delays in providing aid or assistance, and against a charged political backdrop, FEMA and the federal government ulti-mately approved or committed to tens of billions of dollars in aid to Puerto Rico:

- $1.22 billion in individual and household aid
- $3.71 billion in public assistance grants
- $3.45 billion for emergency work
- $680.4 million in housing assistance

The agency said it was the largest, longest, and most unprecedented disaster response in American history.[55] Resident Commissioner González tweeted in September 2018 that Congress thus far had committed to more than $44 bil-lion of aid to Puerto Rico, "with still more to come." It's worth noting that Puerto Rico estimates that its disaster and economic recovery will cost $125 billion in the ten-year period between 2018 and 2028.[56]

Exodus

Many people in Puerto Rico couldn't wait for the snail-paced local or federal response to arrive. They were homeless, they were frightened, they were tired, they were hungry, they were thirsty, and they were sick. Pushing aside personal shock and trauma, the adrenalin kicked in, and tens of thousands of survivors bolted for the exits to ensure their or their family members' safety and survival. Thousands rushed to the airport, seeking to board the first available commercial flights to Florida and other states. But operations were shut down at the San Juan airport, which also had no electricity, food, or running water. When the airport reopened about two days after Maria, only military flights were allowed, which meant people were left to wander the airport desert until commercial flights resumed. Once again, however, Puerto Ricans responded to a crisis by seeking to leave the island, or "jump the pond," accelerating an already histori-cal migration prompted by ten years of a stagnant and painful economy. Just as Puerto Rico is no stranger to hurricanes, the island is also no stranger to migra-tion, for the story of Puerto Rico in the twentieth century is a story of continual migration to the States, known colloquially as the *va y ven*, or the come-and-go.

Others less charitably call it "a dismemberment of the Puerto Rican nation that has yet to run its course."[57] Since the American takeover of Puerto Rico, the island's "problem" often has been defined in Malthusian terms of overpopulation and shortages of food. The Puerto Rican government depended on, even encouraged, population migration as an important valve to relieve economic pressure. Thus, Puerto Rico has experienced three major outmigration flows while under the American flag:

- The Great Migration between 1940 and 1960, in which over 500,000 Puerto Ricans left the island for points north;
- the Millennial Migration between 2013 and 2016 spurred by the economic recession, which sent another 470,000 packing for the States and which converted Florida into a major receiving state;
- and the ongoing Post-Maria Migration, with Florida again in the eye of the migration storm.[58]

Nearly 130,000 Puerto Ricans abandoned the island between July 2017 and July 2018, about 59 percent higher than the 81,500 people who migrated from Puerto Rico in 2017,[59] which is a reflection of stagnant conditions on the island, as well as the people's impatience with government hurricane response, according to the Center for Puerto Rican Studies.[60] Without a doubt, the Post-Maria Migration will continue to erode Puerto Rico's population and tax base, further complicating its economic recovery. Even before Hurricane Maria, Puerto Rico reported that in 2017, for the first time, deaths outnumbered births, a scary development for the island. Younger, working-age people fleeing the island en masse are generating a downward population and economic spiral in Puerto Rico.[61] All told, more than 5.4 million Puerto Ricans live stateside, about 2 million more than on the island.

The Diaspora Is Galvanized

The Puerto Rican diaspora in Florida galvanized on social media to help welcome survivors with open arms. Groups such as Orlando's CASA, a coalition of Latino organizations, amassed 2 million pounds of water and other supplies for Puerto Rico, while Latino Leadership Inc. collected clothing and food, compiled a list of resources for evacuees, and set up a telephone hotline to answer questions.[62] Maria survivors landed in the heart of the new Puerto Rican settlement, particularly Orange and Osceola Counties, areas with the largest concentration of Puerto Ricans in Florida, places that already had been transformed by Puerto Ricans, nearly making the area an extension of Puerto Rico demographically, culturally, and in other ways.[63] They added to the existing dynamic mix of Puerto Ricans from the island and from the diaspora, uniting the two as never before and cementing, for now, the cracks generated by the differing experiences among those born on the island and those born in the States, those who speak Spanish and those who barely speak the language.[64] The Post-Maria Migration is helping to tip the Hispanic population scale in favor of Puerto Ricans, soon to be the largest Hispanic group in Florida, outnumbering Cubans, who have long held that position.[65]

An estimated 53,000 Puerto Ricans migrated to Florida in the six months following the hurricane, according to the Florida Department of Economic and Demographic Research.[66] This represented roughly 42 percent of post-Maria outmigration to the States.[67] More than thirty thousand people displaced by Hurricane Maria sought help from the Multi-Agency Resource Centers at Miami and Orlando airports and the Port of Miami established by then governor Rick Scott, including help with Florida driver's licenses or ID cards, housing, and food stamps.[68] The figure may be imprecise because, while many Puerto Ricans tapped services at these entry points, many others did not, including temporary migrants with no intentions of staying and others taken in by families. Word spread quickly about Florida's Multi-Agency Resource Centers, which opened in October 2017 just two weeks after Maria. Governor Scott declared a state of emergency in all of the state's sixty-seven counties. Florida became an evacuee host state "to assist efforts to provide services to the individuals who have traveled to Florida to escape the devastation."[69] Puerto Ricans made a beeline to the resource centers, where they could find under one roof various state and local agencies, including the state offices of the Federal Emergency Management Agency, the Department of Children and Families, the Department of Highway Safety and Motor Vehicles, the Department of Agriculture and Consumer Services, the Department of Health, the Department of Economic Opportunity (CareerSource), the American Red Cross, and Catholic Charities. Orlando-area organizations included Latino Leadership Inc., Shepherd's Hope, Second Harvest Food Bank, Goodwill, and United Way. Puerto Ricans arriving in Orlando and Miami could leave the airports with a state driver's license or ID card, food, and hotel and transportation vouchers, among other things.

In a series of moves that would further weaken Puerto Rico's hold on its population, particularly professionals, Governor Scott's administration suspended all fees for occupational licenses such as barbers and real estate agents, for Maria evacuees. The state also waived teacher license application fees and transcript requirements, helping to lure more Puerto Rican teachers to Florida. It attracted K–12 students by waiving requirements for documents such as proof of age and a health exam. Florida opened the gates for college students by offering in-state tuition and waiving records requirements, and it pointed out that evacuee students may qualify for funds available to homeless students.[70]

Fueling the Economy

The brunt of the migration came in a flash, but Puerto Ricans arrived in a state well accustomed to experiencing population wave after population wave. The new arrivals are fueling economic growth in a state historically dependent on in-migration for 98 percent of its population expansion. Between 2017 and 2018, Florida's population soared by 357,000, the highest growth in at least six years, magnified by the effects of Hurricane Maria. Puerto Ricans arrived in Florida at a time when the state boasted better than full employment, meaning there were more jobs than workers, signaling that Florida's labor market could absorb the population influx.[71] However, it soon became clear that a bigger issue would be a lack of affordable housing for evacuees, many of whom complained that rents were higher in Florida than in Puerto Rico. Some evacuees said landlords often required up to four thousand dollars to cover first and last months' rents plus a security deposit. Worse, the Florida legislature for the past ten years had raided available affordable housing funds to plug budget holes, hobbling the program. It did so again in fiscal year 2018, even in the face of an evacuee housing crisis.[72] Meanwhile, federal Section 8 housing vouchers were tapped out in many counties, although families could "port" existing vouchers from Puerto Rico to Florida or another state.

Many evacuees had little recourse but to seek temporary housing in hotels and motels under FEMA's Transitional Sheltering Assistance program (TSA). About forty-three states participated in TSA, launched in late December 2017 for Maria evacuees, and by April 2018 the program sheltered 7,856 people. Florida grappled with the largest number of evacuees living in hotels and motels—about 944, more than Puerto Rico's 722.[73] The list of Florida's participating hotels numbered well over one hundred and ran fifteen pages long, ranging from chains such as the Hyatt Regency to the Super 8. Under pressure from states, elected officials, advocacy groups, and evacuee families, FEMA would extend the TSA program seven times, including twice under pressure from the New York–based Puerto Rican civil rights advocacy group LatinoJustice, which filed a class action suit against FEMA.[74] Still, FEMA began placing restrictions on TSA, stating in March 2018 that only people already in the program could continue, disqualifying people living with family and friends or whose homes were undergoing temporary repair under the island's emergency rebuilding program.[75] Several months later, in May, FEMA began offering one-way tickets to Puerto Rico for people who wished to return, but it was not a popular option. By mid-September 2018, only 592 individuals across the States had taken up FEMA's offer, according to the agency. In September 2018, nearly a year after the hurricane struck, the TSA program finally came to an end. However, each time a deadline loomed, fewer and fewer families remained in hotels, so that by then about 298 Florida families were affected by the program's close. The entire program, covering Maria evacuees in 40 states, cost more than $104 million by the time it closed.[76]

Strangely, Puerto Rico's Governor Rosselló never activated FEMA's direct-lease program for evacuees in the States, although he did so for hurricane survivors in Puerto Rico. The direct-lease program would have provided up to eighteen months of rental assistance. The governor openly worried about the throng of migrants leaving the island after Maria, and in June, on a visit to a large Orlando Hispanic church, he pleaded with evacuees to return to the island. "There is only 1 percent without power. Reconstruction funds will reach Puerto Rico, and that will help us improve housing, roads and education," he said. To sweeten the pot, he said the Puerto Rico government would pay for plane tickets and evacuees would be given housing priority.[77]

Political Opportunities

Although there was a severe shortage of housing, political opportunities abounded. The precarious situation of post-Maria migrants provided Governor Rosselló and Florida activists a political opportunity to mine. Rosselló, disappointed in provisions of the federal tax reform that disadvantaged Puerto Rico, announced a get-out-the-vote effort in January 2018 aimed at the Puerto Rican diaspora in hopes of influencing that year's midterm elections. With only one nonvoting member in Congress, Puerto Rico turned to the diaspora with access to the ballot box to raise its collective voice on behalf of Puerto Rico, as many island administrations have done in the past. "We will analyze those who turned their back on Puerto Rico," Governor Rosselló said. "It's crystal clear that because we don't have that direct representation, we're going to have surrogate voices, whether it's Puerto Ricans who moved to the U.S., or the Latino community in general. . . . With a million of us already here and 250,000 more arriving in the last two months [sic], I would imagine that would be enough political pressure."

As the midterms drew nearer, Florida advocates and activists, such as UnidosUS, Hispanic Federation, and Power for Puerto Rico on the national front and Vamos4PuertoRico, Iniciativa Acción Puertorriqueña, and Mi Familia Vota in the Orlando area, pushed evacuees to register to vote and cast a ballot in the August 2018 primaries. Registration rolls climbed, up by 2 percent in Orange County, with Hispanics representing 25 percent of all voters, and 3 percent higher in Osceola County, where Hispanics comprised 48 percent of the electorate.[78] Some evacuees did vote, but with mixed feelings, saying they didn't know enough about Florida politics and/or felt pressured to vote. In either case, Rosselló's voter initiative, called Poder Puerto Rico, was a bust, at least in the midterm primaries, as central Florida organizations complained that the administration didn't follow up.[79] Not to be deterred, however, LatinoJustice successfully sued the state to provide bilingual ballots in the Florida counties that did not have them.[80] The timing of the decision meant that only sample bilingual ballots were provided, but in 2019 a Latino coalition returned to the issue, asking a federal court to require greater bilingual voter assistance, including bilingual ballots, in time for the 2019 and 2020 elections.[81] Newly elected Florida governor Ron DeSantis responded positively, stating: "Florida has a significant Spanish-speaking population and our state is home to many Puerto Ricans who moved here after the devastation of Hurricane Maria. These fellow citizens should be able to fully participate in our democracy." DeSantis ordered the state's supervisors of elections to address voting accessibility issues.[82]

Efforts to convert Puerto Ricans into active voters are hot and ongoing in the swing state of Florida, which regularly turns shades of red to blue and back again in election cycles. The political impact, however, remains to be

seen. Although Puerto Rico governor Rosselló endorsed Democratic US senator Bill Nelson for reelection in the 2018 midterm election, many Puerto Ricans voted for Republican governor Rick Scott, who ousted Nelson. In fact,
in an early 2019 poll of Puerto Ricans in Florida, 48 percent, or nearly half,
of respondents gave Scott the highest favorability ranking of any elected official, including US senator Marco Rubio, US representative Darren Soto, and
then Puerto Rico governor Rosselló.[83] That is likely due to Scott's high profile
among Puerto Ricans in the aftermath of Hurricane Maria.

Lasting Effects

The lasting effects of the new migrants on the Florida diaspora, itself a unique
mix of Puerto Ricans from Puerto Rico and first, second, and third generations
from various states, continue to unfold. In today's hurry-up-and-get-over-it
world, newcomers have been caricatured as freeloaders, and empathy for their
plight has run out. Sympathy shifted to other disasters: Hurricane Florence in
September 2018 and Hurricane Michael in October 2018. An *Orlando Sentinel*
letter writer quoted Benjamin Franklin on the benefits of self-sufficiency and
admonished, "People need to pick themselves up by their bootstraps and move
on." The lack of empathy is not only stateside, for a commenter in Puerto
Rico's largest newspaper, *El Nuevo Día*, wrote: "I don't know how these people
have lived one year for free and couldn't even look for jobs. As a Puerto Rican
I am embarrassed. Go to work. Enough sucking on that pacifier."[84] Yet, disasters tend to produce post-traumatic stress disorder (PTSD) and other mental
health issues among survivors, particularly the poor or vulnerable, even a
year or more after the event. In a Puerto Rico Department of Education Medical University of South Carolina survey of more than 96,000 schoolchildren
conducted five to nine months after the storm, about 7 percent were found
to have "clinically significant symptoms of PTSD," with girls more affected
than boys by a full percentage point.[85] The findings are in keeping with other
posthurricane studies. As many as twelve or more months after Hurricane
Katrina, for instance, certain survivors experienced poor mental and physical
health, as well as PTSD.[86] The Medical University of South Carolina warned
that although previous studies have shown that half of children adjust and
recover within a year of a natural disaster, up to one-third will develop chronic

symptoms such as post-traumatic stress disorder, depression, anxiety, and substance abuse, among other behaviors.[87]

In light of such information, the University of Central Florida opened the UCF Restores Clinic to combat PTSD, depression and anxiety, or marital problems among Puerto Rican families displaced by Hurricanes Maria and Irma, located in the Episcopal Church of Jesus of Nazareth of Orlando, which played a major role in assisting Hurricane Maria evacuees. The program, part of an earlier initiative that provides mental health services to veterans, aims to assist one hundred people in a year. (See the interview with Father José Rodríguez in chapter 5, "The View from Orlando." Also, *Tossed to the Wind* collaborator Nancy Rosado is affiliated with UCF Restores.)[88]

After the initial rush of response to the accelerated hurricane migration, cracks among the Florida diaspora began to appear. Some pre-Maria migrants complained that more established Puerto Ricans were complacent about helping the new arrivals, making the forging of a cohesive Puerto Rican community a challenge.[89] After the hurricane, a University of Miami study found that survivors who moved to central Florida didn't feel as welcomed as those who settled in south Florida, hindering their efforts to settle in.[90] The complaints carry some weight, as Florida's pre-Maria Puerto Rican community was likelier to have lower unemployment, higher incomes, and was significantly less likely to live in poverty compared with recent movers.[91] Maria may have widened the gap. How to bridge the divide between the different Puerto Rican diasporas will be a topic of much future discussion and, hopefully, research for years to come. It may be a while, likely after the 2020 US census, before an accurate sociodemographic profile of post-Maria migrants can be compiled, but it's safe to say that the Puerto Rican diaspora has always been fluid, redefined by each wave of migrants over many decades. In Florida, the diaspora is a confluence of rivers of people born in Puerto Rico and those born in the States, very different from the diaspora of the mid-twentieth century to the Northeast. Drilling down, in central Florida, unlike in New York, the island-born diaspora and the Spanish tongue already predominated before the Maria migration began.[92] It's possible that the posthurricane migrants may double-down on the notion of Puerto Ricans as transnational people, leading dual lives—belonging here in the States and there in Puerto Rico—creating dual identities and expressing dual loyalties to each.[93]

Migrant Voices

Whether *aquí* or *allá*, here or there, post-Maria migrants' stories deserve to be documented and heard, for this population has endured real, ongoing, and lasting trauma as a result of this singular event in the history of Puerto Rico. Thousands of stories have been written, published, and broadcast about Hurricane Maria survivors, both those living in Puerto Rico and those who moved to Florida. Even so, it's hard to get a solid sense of the humanity and complexity of the individuals who endured the powerful storm. This book is an attempt to remedy that, to provide a voice for migrants, for they look very much like many other longtime Puerto Rican residents of the Orlando area with deep roots on the island. Maria evacuees are our family, friends, and new neighbors. Except that, unlike in previous migration waves, many Maria migrants carry a deep sense of trauma and loss. It is important to preserve their stories as part of the history of the Puerto Rican community in central Florida but, just as important, to do so for the sake of posterity. Future generations should be able to read the personal stories not as clinical accounts of yet another Puerto Rican migration but as the tales of people who made tough, even brave, decisions under the most trying of circumstances.

The survivors who tell their stories in *Tossed to the Wind* were allowed the luxury of telling their tales from beginning to end, to place the storm within the contexts of their daily lives and routines. The interviewees left an indelible impression. The glue that held the survivors together was their remarkable resilience, offering hope and optimism for the future. *Tossed to the Wind* captures these stories in the survivors' own words and voices, before the burden and heaviness of remembrance is gone. Before they, too, begin to doubt their own recollections, before they begin to question: "Did that really happen? Did I really do that? Maybe I'm misremembering. It's all so blurry now." Readers will get a clearer idea of how ordinary people faced down extraordinary circumstances. Maybe they'll understand how tens of thousands of Puerto Ricans came to be tossed to the wind by Hurricane Maria, generating a spur-of-the-moment migration of unprecedented proportions. Please stop for a moment and pay attention, for their gentle breath "my sails must fill, or else my project fails."[94]

2

TELLING SURVIVORS' STORIES

The fifteen interviewees in *Tossed to the Wind* were chosen because they represent various circumstances and people thrust by Hurricane Maria into a twilight zone of desperation but also of resistance and resilience. The baseline motivation for the interviews was to hear more, much more, about what happened. We wanted answers to such questions as, "Who are the survivors?" and, "What exactly happened to them during and after the storm?" We wanted to understand the whole story, not just bits and pieces as printed in newspapers or broadcast in thirty-second sound bites on the evening news. We wanted to place a face on Hurricane Maria survivors so that future generations could understand that the onrush of Puerto Ricans to the States, particularly Florida, was no ordinary migration but a concentrated, once-in-a-lifetime event of historical proportions—an event that changed not only Puerto Rico but also the communities in which hurricane survivors settled.

Finding survivors was easy but also difficult. The newcomers were all around us in Florida, the preferred migration spot for Puerto Ricans even before the hurricane. Since the storm more than 50,000 have settled in Florida out of between 150,000 and 175,000 who fled the devastated island in the year after Hurricane Maria.[1] We knew where to find people who were living in hotels and motels, for many were concentrated along Highway 192 in Kissimmee, according to news reports. We found all of the hotel-based evacuees by making cold calls. No formal introductions, no scientific or demographic calculations. We visited the hotels and literally knocked on doors asking to interview people, asking them to trust us with their stories. To our astonishment, survivors let us in and talked with us for hours, allowing us to take photos and videos for this project. They also directed us to others in the hotel who might be interested in participating. Soon, the Baymont Inn became our preferred hotel. That is where we found and interviewed during multiple visits, in order: Rosa Then Ortiz, Sugeilly Meléndez, Miriam Echevarría and José Antonio Vázquez, Wilda Cirino, and Dacny Segarra. David Olmeda was the first hotel evacuee we spoke with, but he was staying at a Super 8 motel, also along Highway 192.

We did not advertise, so to speak, to find any evacuee. One person led to another and then another. We worked our extensive circle of central Florida friends, contacts, and acquaintances. That's how we landed the interview with Rebecca Colón, a teacher recommended by a teacher-friend. Father José Rodríguez, who aided many evacuees, also came to us via several recommendations. More important, we searched for survivors where they might be. In addition to visiting hotels, we attended welcome or orientation workshops for Hispanic newcomers. That is where we found Ivelisse Marrero as well as José Cruz Vázquez and Yatmarie Negrón Ocasio. We found Jorge Olivero Pagán, whose evacuee family lived with him in Orlando for nearly a year, working at a restaurant. When he began telling his story, it generated the idea to include relatives and activists who were on the receiving end of the hurricane migration. What was that like?

We wanted to interview a gamut of Puerto Rican survivors—females, males, families, single mothers, singles, the elderly, students, the disabled, the sick or ill, working-class people and professionals, a business owner, understanding that their experiences would be different. We succeeded on most counts, but disappointingly we were not successful in interviewing every person contacted. Although we reached out to dozens of people, the fifteen stories of Hurricane Maria survivors in this book represent the most solid interviews with the greatest detail. The survivors spoke to us in their hotel rooms or homes, sometimes over coffee. One interviewee had little furniture, so we sat on the floor. Evacuees were often apprehensive about the interview, growing more relaxed as the "chat" unfolded, laughing and even crying over their experiences. We were clear that each person gifted us with their words and every tear they shed. Some were genuinely relieved to relate their experiences, undergoing a form of catharsis. Many confessed that they hadn't spoken of the entire ordeal before. One survivor insisted we join hands in a prayer circle by the end of the interview.

But not surprisingly, some survivors didn't want to be interviewed for various reasons, including not wanting to relive the trauma of the hurricane. For instance, finding a business owner proved unfruitful. One person didn't want to be interviewed, while another was establishing a location for a Puerto Rico business and was not a survivor. One student was eager to talk about his hurricane experience but canceled the interview under family pressure. Still others didn't respond to calls and emails, even after the initial in-person contact. On our end, we politely declined a few who volunteered to be interviewed because they didn't meet the definition of a Hurricane Maria survivor; for example, they might have arrived in Florida before the hurricane. Excluding partial interviews and people who didn't meet the project's criteria, the book includes exactly the number of survivors interviewed at length and whom we felt formed a mosaic of Hurricane Maria survivors: fifteen. All but two chose to be interviewed in Spanish, their native tongue.

The interviews were recorded on Apple 6 and 7 smartphones and also video and audio equipment to create backup systems. Nancy was in charge of the audio and video recordings while also taking photos during the interview sessions. It was important to be informal during the interviews so as not to add to the pressure survivors were under and, just as important, not to stanch the flow of words. As the primary interviewer, I initially was a bit too eager, making the mistake of holding the smartphone intimidatingly close to the interviewees, some of whom recoiled. Subsequently, I held the phone down and more out of sight. In addition, I soon set aside a list of prepared questions that made the interviews feel stilted and unnatural, as if I were reading from a script, which of course I was. Instead, I let the interviews flow while still following the general outline of questions. This boosted eye contact—and trust.

List of Questions

Bio
- Name
- Age/occupation
- Town of origin
- Who did you live with?

Hurricanes

- How did Hurricane Irma affect you?
- How did that prepare you for Hurricane Maria?
- What did you expect of Maria?
- What actually happened to you during Hurricane Maria?
- What did you do before and during the storm?
- Who were you with?
- When did you get the idea this was a serious storm?
- When did you know the storm was over?
- What happened to you or your relatives?
- What happened to your home or property?

Post-Maria

- Did you have water or electricity?
- Did you ask for government help?
- When did you know you had to leave?
- Did you have any doubts about leaving?
- How did you prepare to leave?
- What was the last thing you did before leaving?
- Did you bring any special memento with you as a reminder of home or family?

Stateside

- When did you leave Puerto Rico?
- How did you arrive in Florida?
- Why Florida?
- Who picked you up from the airport?
- Where did you initially stay?
- What was the first thing you did?
- Did you use the resource center?

Long-Term

- What are you doing now?
- What is your long-term goal?
- Do you think of returning to the island? Why or why not?

I simultaneously translated and transcribed each interview, listening to the stories of suffering and survival, not just once but again and again, hitting "forward" and "back" on the audio and video recordings to get it right. The stories were edited for clarity and to reduce or eliminate repetition.

After all was said, this is what we came up with—a remarkable collection of firsthand accounts of Hurricane Maria in Puerto Rico. Following, in full, are the stories of fifteen survivors of Puerto Rico's Hurricane Maria.

3

LIVING IN HOTELS

The overwhelming majority of post-Maria migrants to Florida and other states did not stay in hotels. Of the hundreds of thousands of Puerto Ricans who fled the island to the States after the hurricane, about eight thousand survivors across forty-three states enrolled in FEMA's Transitional Sheltering Assistance program, or TSA, which was launched about a month after the September storm.[1] Many but not all Maria survivors with TSA vouchers stayed at hotels near Highway 192 in Kissimmee, in the shadow of Walt Disney World. The hotel dwellers were the first to be politicized, as every three months the deadline that might yank their housing assistance vouchers hovered overhead. Many worked with advocacy groups and held press conferences calling attention to their plight. For better or for worse, survivors living in temporary quarters became the public and dominant face of Hurricane Maria evacuees. What follows are the stories of six families living in hotels, the majority at the Baymont Inn in Kissimmee.

Dacny Segarra

It's a monster.

Dacny Segarra, fifty-two, and Alfredo Quintero, fifty-four, arrived in Orlando from Río Piedras, Puerto Rico, on November 28, 2017, along with twelve family members, including two sons, two daughters, a son-in-law and daughter-in-law, and six grandchildren ages fourteen, twelve, ten, nine, eight, and four. Since arriving in Florida, the family, whose Puerto Rico house partially collapsed, has been living in hotel rooms, first in Orlando and later at the Baymont Inn in Kissimmee. Her children were job hunting at the time of the interview, and they hoped to rent a single-family home or buy a mobile home where they could live together as before.

We're from Río Piedras, Puerto Rico, Barrio Tortugo, which is part of the Caimito sector of Río Piedras. I'm here with my husband, Alfredo Quintero, fifty-four, who is disabled and in a wheelchair. My husband and children were the ones who prepared for the hurricanes because I had blood clots in my leg, and I spent both hurricanes in the hospital. I was able to perceive the hurricane winds through the hospital window, although I didn't hear anything. My children tell me the wind was very strong, like a monster, especially Maria. I couldn't get out of bed, and it was very difficult because I had a second blood clot and was taken to a second hospital for an operation. When I left the hospital at the end of September 2017, I saw total destruction. It was incredible. Everything was destroyed.

We inherited our house from my grandmother. It is a three-level house. I lived on the third floor; my father, who is seventy-nine years old, and my mother, who is seventy-two, still live on the second floor. My daughter lived on the bottom floor with her two children. We had to leave the house because FEMA inspectors said the house was dangerous. The rain had come down hard, two trees fell down—*flamboyán* and *quenepa* trees—and that caused the land to become soft. A sinkhole opened up behind the first floor, and the house was

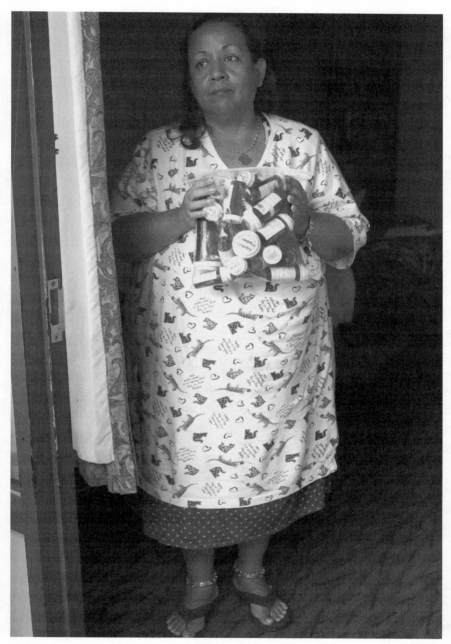

Dacny Segarra

in danger of collapsing. A neighbor's tree split and fell on top of my house, but a DIRECTV® antenna kept the tree from hitting the house. The hurricane was so strong it brought beach sand with the water. My windows went flying, and the water came in, mixed with sand. Later, when I opened the drawers of the dresser, the clothes were soaked, and they smelled like the ocean. In the back of the house there was a hillside and creek that had been lush and dense. Now you could see everything, even the dirt. Many wood homes were gone. My husband spent the hurricane locked in a room with our two grandchildren because they were scared of the noise. They started crying, telling their grandfather, "It's a monster." According to what my children told me, my son Wilfredo and my daughter Dacny tried to open the front door, and the wind was so strong they fell on their backs. A neighbor Antonio—God bless him, he was raised with my children—had a generator. In the middle of the hurricane, he and my son connected my husband's sleep apnea machine to the generator. We lived through Hurricanes Hugo and Georges, but this was totally different. Hugo and Georges were strong hurricanes and destroyed property. Irma prepared the path for Maria, and Maria destroyed everything. Even the walls and pillars of cement houses cracked. That's how strong it was.

After the hurricane, it was difficult to get gasoline, candles, water. Sometimes you would go to the supermarket and the shelves were empty. The help we were supposed to get didn't arrive as promised. While I was in the hospital, military people came to the house and gave us cases of military food when they saw that my husband was in a wheelchair and after he explained that there were many of us. They gave out envelopes with dried food: vegetables, bread, peanut butter, juice—all in brown envelopes because that's the food the military eats. They gave us many cases of food so that when I left the hospital, we ate that food. On one occasion—and thank God I was in the hospital—they killed an iguana. We call it *gallina de palo* in Puerto Rico. One of my sons killed it, and my daughter, she's a chef, she prepared it, skinning and cutting it into pieces to make a *fricasé*. They said it tasted like chicken, but I never would have eaten it. I get panicky when I see a lizard. How am I going to eat an iguana? Many other people had it worse. The city of San Juan—our area is part of San Juan—was supposed to send us aid. After I left the hospital, they gave us groceries on only two occasions, but I heard on the news that there were pallets of water and food in the Hiram Bithorn Stadium, and they didn't distribute it. When night would fall, it was silent—silent in terms of the people because the generators made noise all night long. There was a neighbor who had two generators and ran them day and night, so much so that the noise would get into your head. We had flashlights and candles, but we couldn't use them all the time. The batteries would die, and then it was difficult to find batteries. So we would sit in the *balcón,* or sometimes I would lie in bed in total darkness. The darkness doesn't bother me, but the heat was another thing. After the hurricane it was hot; then came the mosquitoes. At that time my daughter worked in Applebee's, and she would bring ice to me, my parents, and for herself. Every night she brought ice because Applebee's said she could.

We had been thinking of coming to Florida, but the hurricane really motivated us to leave. My husband was the one who decided we should leave. FEMA didn't pay our airfare. My husband bought and paid for tickets for all of us on the internet. He gave us a month to prepare our suitcases little by little. I couldn't do much because I had just come out of the hospital. I packed seven suitcases because I came to establish myself, and I couldn't leave my *batas* [women's shifts] behind. I still have things in my house that I couldn't bring, but when I get my own place I will send for the things I left behind. We arrived here on November 28 [2017]. I'm here with my four children, two girls and two boys, two sons/daughters-in-law and six grandchildren. We are fourteen. The first night we stayed in a hotel that my husband found. It looked perfect on the internet, but when we arrived it was next to a jail, and there were people selling drugs. We had a corner room, and in the hallway that's what you saw. I arrived with all my jewelry because I have a lot of gold jewelry. That night we heard knocks on our window all night, and I told my son Wilfredo: "Don't you dare open the window. That's what they want. They want to rob us." Because of that scare I took off all my jewelry and put it away. Now I only wear silver.

The room smelled of cigarettes. You couldn't step on the rug. I had on sandals, and I was dying to take them off and put on slippers. When I touched the floor it was sticky and black. The air-conditioning wasn't working. We had arrived at midnight, so we couldn't leave. But the next day I quickly called our cousin—we have some family here—and said I was scared. We found another hotel a little further down, where we spent seven days. My husband was going to continue paying, but on the seventh day the hotel said we had to leave. Desperate to find another place, my daughter got on the phone until she found this hotel from a FEMA list. I can't complain about this hotel. I can't complain about the housekeeping or the owners. They have all been good to us. Even though the rooms are not equipped for cooking, they allow us to cook in each room. They reasoned that we had left a country that was destroyed with little money and we can't buy restaurant food with the little money we have. They have been very aware of our situation. We also have a continental breakfast. It's very simple, but we have a breakfast. I say that it has been excellent. I can't complain about anything. They are always paying attention to our needs. It's not like other places I've heard about that don't provide the service they're supposed to. A church is also helping us, an Episcopal church. They sent a social worker, who gave us a voucher for groceries, and those were real groceries—oil, rice, beans, milk, spaghetti, juice for the kids. The other food we received was canned. We left canned food behind in Puerto Rico!

We've been here five months already, and we have to leave. We have dealt with two Realtors who have been sincere, and each has told us that there is a conspiracy in Florida between homeowners and Realtors not to rent to *boricuas* [Puerto Ricans]. The reason they supposedly give is that Puerto Ricans break things and don't pay. But we're not all like that. Why are they characterizing all of us the same way? We recently went to Apopka to see if we can buy a mobile home. They are asking for a deposit of only $2,774. But other places have demanded income that is three times the rent. If your rent is $1,400, that comes to over $4,000. They ask for the first month's rent, a month of deposit, and the last month's rent. In reality, of the three months they are asking for, one is for the Realtor. That's another problem. The Realtors have a monopoly. When you apply for a house, they don't tell you if there are ten or fifteen other applications. Even when they know you don't qualify because of your income, they ask you to fill out an application and leave a deposit, which is money they don't return to you. We almost lost money. A Realtor asked us for $350, but the day we were to make the deposit I thank God that it was raining, and there was a traffic jam. The Realtor left the house. When my husband called her, she said she couldn't deal with irresponsible people, and the next time we would have to give her $400 because her time was worth gold. Other Realtors warned us to be careful because some were scamming people. You give them money, and then they disappear. This is the system.

There is also racism. That's why I don't answer calls if I don't recognize the number. I received one call, and he spoke to me in English. I said in my poor English that I didn't speak English; I spoke Spanish. He said to me very clearly, "Thank God I don't speak Spanish" and hung up. So you see, there's also racism. We *boricuas* are not used to that, we *boricuas* accept everyone equally. We're not looking to see if you're black or white, if you're Mexican or Venezuelan or Dominican. We don't discriminate like that toward anyone; then you come here and you're confronted with it. There are some Americans who notice you're Latino and speak Spanish, and they are bothered by it. We're not used to this, and it depresses you. The church has sent us to other Realtors, but they all demand the same thing. They are not giving us any consideration. We left Puerto Rico because it was destroyed. We want to establish ourselves. We want to live here. We want to get ahead. We didn't come here on vacation. We came here to establish ourselves. They are not understanding that. This situation is depressing, and I already suffer from depression. I have to control myself and have faith in God that soon we will be able to have something so we can move from here. We didn't come here for others to support us all the time. That's not our motive; that's not what we want. What we need is a push, an opportunity to continue forward. FEMA is not going to give us any more housing extensions. There are fourteen of us. Where are we going to go? We're not looking for an apartment because there are a lot of us. We need a house. We want to stay together because we have always been together. I am like a mother hen with chickadees under my wings. I've always been like that. I won't leave any of my children behind.

One person alone is not going to be able to make it. We have known single people who have solicited an apartment, and they are demanding they have two jobs to meet the income limit. We're supposed to have four thousand dollars a month in income. From where? Jobs don't pay so much as to have a four-thousand-dollar income. That's impossible. My son Wilfredo still hasn't found a job. My oldest son, Alfredo, is a barber, and he is earning some money. My youngest daughter is disabled. She hurt her back and can't work, but her husband works. My oldest daughter was working, but they weren't giving her many hours. She also was getting food stamps, but they took away the food stamps. I recommended she leave the job because her daughter is a little sick and needs her. I couldn't take care of her. Her husband then found a second job working as a dishwasher. They each bought used vans, the same model and the same year, but one is blue and one is gray. At least we have transportation. There are some who don't have anything to move around with.

We are not well in terms of health. I'm supposed to be taking a medication for life called Xarelto®, and I have the letters of proof from my doctor stating that I need to take the medication because I am at risk of getting blood clots. Right now, I am not taking any medicine. The thing is, it costs six hundred dollars, which we don't have. I can't pay for it. In Puerto Rico I used to get it for free. My legs were swollen recently for two weeks. My husband has kidney failure, heart problems—he has a pacemaker—and had one leg amputated below the knee. He is diabetic. He was in an accident, cut his leg, and it caught an infection. He has one glass eye, and the other one has had laser surgery. His health is delicate. He's already been hospitalized here two times. A doctor visits him once a month, and a nurse comes once a week. The doctors say he is on borrowed time. He is in God's hands. When we landed here we didn't get Medicaid or food stamps because since he is disabled and we don't pay rent, we don't qualify. There's a limit of $1,025 in income per month in order to receive aid, and he gets $1,091 in Social Security disability. That's not enough to live on here.

There are groups that want to help us and congressmen too. It's not all blah, blah, blah, as we *boricuas* like to say. It's also about doing, to fulfill what they promise. A congressman came here and said he was fighting to extend the housing vouchers for one year because there is no housing; there are no apartments. But that hasn't happened. Our hands are tied. My husband jokes and laughs, but it's a way to keep from getting depressed. He says we'll go to Walmart and buy some tents and live in tents until we can get something. I hope to God that we can find at least a mobile home with three bedrooms to accommodate us. I don't care if it's small. The point is to have a roof, to stabilize ourselves and push forward. FEMA has come to the hotels to tell us that they will pay for our tickets back to Puerto Rico. Some have returned because of the pressure and the inability to find something. But in our case, when they came we told them no. They have sent three different people three different times. They told us we have until June 30 to decide in order for FEMA to pay the return tickets to Puerto Rico. But FEMA didn't pay for our tickets to come here. We paid for those tickets. We paid for the first week in hotels until we heard that there was help available to stay in hotels. I cannot return to Puerto

Rico. I love my island. I love and miss my island. I miss my parents, my sister, my nieces and nephews—I miss my family. But the situation in Puerto Rico is not good. We have opportunities here.

The first thing Wilfredo did was to find a baseball team for his son. Now he's in a baseball team, practicing from Monday through Thursday, and Wilfredo is the coach. They recently played in a tournament. He met a professional baseball player from the Atlanta Braves who gave him a pair of batters' gloves. He told my grandson, "You earned it. *Este chichí batea.*" This little one can hit. The change in him has been from night to day. We want to stay here because of our grandchildren and the schools. Sometimes I feel like I'm on the outside. Sometimes you get desperate because there's little time left. We are searching, we are looking. We prefer to buy a place. Let's see what happens. We came here blindly, but I would do everything the same again because, despite everything, we want to move forward. Why go back? The schools are worse. The health system has worsened. The water and electricity rates went up. Everything has gone up. I compare the prices here and there, and it's much less expensive here. If we went back in time we would make the same decision: come here, establish ourselves, push ahead, especially for our grandchildren.

David Olmeda

This is the moment to get out.

David Olmeda, twenty-six, was staying at the Super 8 motel in Kissimmee, Florida, with his wife, Christine González, twenty-six, and his sixteen-month-old son, Kahil David. He arrived from Cayey, Puerto Rico, in November 2017 and within two weeks found part-time work at a Home Depot, unloading merchandise from trucks and stocking inventory on shelves. He had been a truck driver in Puerto Rico. Since arriving in Orlando, Olmeda experienced a political awakening, participating in demonstrations and speaking out on behalf of Puerto Ricans stuck in hotels.

David Olmeda with his partner, Christine González, and son, Kahil David

We rented an apartment made of wood with a zinc roof in Cayey, Puerto Rico, so it was a weak structure. We knew the hurricane was going to be super-intense so my mother-in-law asked that we stay with her. As the hurricane passed, we looked out the window and could see the winds were strong. I thought, wow, what must be happening to our apartment at this moment. We had left all our things inside. But our main concern was to remain calm because there were two families living in one house now. The storm ripped the skylights off my mother-in-law's house, and in the middle of the hurricane we were mopping up water with towels. We had to invent ways to contain the water because it was coming in through the ceiling. The hurricane passed at night. When day came and we could see out, everything was destruction. I knew then that our apartment had to be completely destroyed. We lost everything—the baby's crib, his clothes. We had no choice but to move into my mother-in-law's house.

I was working as a trucker in Puerto Rico and spent two weeks without work because my truck's lift and cables were damaged, plus you couldn't find diesel gasoline. When I finally started to work, the lines at my job were super, kilometers-long* since there was no electricity, no computer, no generators. It was a very difficult situation. We didn't know what to do. As they say in Puerto Rico, we had water up to our necks. There were a lot of things happening—the lines to get food, to get gas, to get ice. We asked ourselves, "Why is all this happening at the same time?" My mother-in-law gave us a hand because we couldn't do much. She helped us unconditionally. We didn't receive any other aid. People commented, "Look, there's food at the docks," but that turned out to be another problem. There were trailerloads arriving, and they couldn't get them out for lack of personnel. On the radio they made a call for truckers to go to the docks in San Juan and Guaynabo, but when we got there they asked us to sign in because there was a waiting list and to wait our turn to be called. There were a lot of people who wanted to help the country. I heard about a person who arrived at the docks with his wife and a fleet of trucks and offered to move all the merchandise for only the price of diesel, and he was told, "Okay, wait your turn." They never called him. What was happening in that moment? Where was the money that was arriving for friends and relatives while people were experiencing deprivations and were still trapped inside their homes? Where's the money that celebrities donated? The food they donated? We don't know of any food or money that reached the people. All the millions arriving on the island was to build homes for the people who had lost everything. We never found out what happened; we never heard of any money the government gave for this or that. I am angry at the government of Puerto Rico. What did they do with all the millions sent to Puerto Rico? Who did they give it to? I didn't see any help given out. What else can I think?

I was uncomfortable with this, since people were lacking basic necessities; they were experiencing hunger. I had to check on my parents and my daughter—I have a four-year-old daughter from a previous marriage. I am over here on the street, but do you know what I would give to be with my daughter at this moment? I got here because a friend, Pablo Hernández

---

* The unit of distance measurement in Puerto Rico is the kilometer.

in Orlando, asked me to check on his mom in Puerto Rico who had been recently operated on. He was concerned because he hadn't heard from her. I went to see her, and she was in bad shape. She said, "I feel ill, I'm dizzy, and I don't have transportation to get to the hospital." Pablo offered her a plane ticket, but at the time the airport was not operating. Flights were being canceled, and there were long lines inside the terminals. Two weeks after she arrived in Florida, she offered to help me if I came, saying, "I know things are not that easy over there." I took a month to decide since I was working as a trucker, getting up at 2:00 a.m. and going to the factory to wait my turn to deliver merchandise. Before the hurricane I worked at least five days a week, but after the hurricane I was working only two to three days a week. That's not enough to support my family, plus provide child support for my daughter. Many people cannot live so long without food, electricity, and gasoline. I said to my wife, "This is the moment to get out." There was nothing for us in Puerto Rico. I would go first to my friend Pablo's house and look for work. I wanted to get her and my son out of there.

I had been to Florida two times before. In 2013 I spent two weeks here vacationing with my family, and in 2015 I was here for nearly three weeks. I liked Florida and its environment. I thought, "Wow, I love it here." There's a warmth here, and sometimes here and there you find other Puerto Ricans. It was a good environment. I couldn't complain. But it's not the same to come to Florida for vacation as it is to come here to live. Nothing is the same. When I arrived in Florida I stayed with Pablo from November to February. Then my wife and me received money from FEMA to replace some of the things we had lost. She bought airplane tickets and came with my son because we had been told we were eligible for aid. We came straight to this motel because it is close to my job. I had no transportation at the time, and Home Depot is a twenty-minute walk. I walked every day going and coming, and sometimes my supervisor would offer a lift. I work from nine at night to six in the morning, and they pay me twelve dollars an hour. Sometimes I work twenty-four hours a week, sometimes thirty or forty hours a week. I started at eleven dollars an hour, and right now I'm waiting to be interviewed for a promotion to go full-time. When I get off work I come here, and my wife goes to work. In other words, we're not waiting for people to place things in our hands. We are not, as Puerto Ricans say, sitting around fanning ourselves. I am working and hustling for what's mine. There are a lot of people who say we are parasites. Some people left Facebook comments after we protested in front of PRFAA [the Puerto Rican Federal Affairs Administration]. They said we're lazy; they said we think we can coast all our lives, that it's time for us to move on. It's not like that. We're not all parasites. I'm not spending my time at Disney. We're trying to move forward. We didn't come here to be maintained by the public. Like I said at the demonstration, we just need a little push because we have searched for an apartment and everything's full. We are working and hustling for what's ours. We don't want anything handed to us.

I can't complain being here at the Super 8. We have neighbors who are Puerto Ricans who also were affected by Hurricane Maria. We are always in communication—talking, commenting on what's happening, and exchanging information. Many of us joined a support group called Vamos4Puerto Rico [which arranged the protests in front of PRFAA]. I didn't expect to spend this much time in a motel. In my mind I thought we'd be here three months, but the apartment waiting lists are long. This week the motel people knocked on our doors saying the FEMA housing voucher would expire and we had to move out. My wife called FEMA, and they said there will be an extension. The next day FEMA called back and said, "No, there will be no extension." They're telling people different things. They create the expectation that we have a little more time to find an apartment. But what they're doing is playing with our emotions. I don't have any family in this state, none at all. I can't go back with my friend Pablo. I can't go back to Puerto Rico. I have nothing in Puerto Rico. I can't go back to live with my mother-in-law. She has her own lifestyle; my father has his own lifestyle. Everything is different. I can't go back to start from zero, without jobs. My plan is to find a cheaper motel that I can pay until I find an apartment. I can try to negotiate with the Super 8 to lower their price, although I don't know what we pay. The money goes directly from FEMA to the Super 8. All of us here are trying to encourage each other because none of us wants to be out on the street. Let's see what happens.

I brought only a few things when I came to Florida. I didn't pack or prepare for the situation I am going through. I can't say I prepared myself emotionally either. I thought, okay, I'm going to the United States to get a job, but everything has turned out so difficult. I have my memories of Puerto

Rico. I haven't seen my parents who are still in Cayey, and my daughter doesn't understand what's happening. When I call she asks, "Papá when are you coming?" I think Puerto Ricans downplayed the hurricane. They said, "No, the hurricane is not coming, the hurricane is not coming." Others said, "If the hurricane is coming, then let it come." I think Puerto Ricans are too trusting. We have to remain vigilant and plan for these things, not take it as a joke. The great lesson in all of this has been that when it's your turn, it's your turn. The thing to do is to prepare yourself, take security measures, although either way my apartment would have been destroyed. If people had paid more attention to the news warning—to prepare ourselves—maybe things wouldn't have turned out so bad.

Rosa Then Ortiz

My nerves were bad, and my husband was so sick.

Rosa Then Ortiz, a seventy-seven-year-old retiree, is from Guánica, Puerto Rico, on the southern coast. She and her husband, Cruz Then Lorenzo, seventy-five years old and disabled, to whom she's been married for forty-eight years, arrived in the Orlando area on December 27, 2017, with an adult daughter, a teacher. Then Ortiz lived for a time in New York from age thirteen, and much later she also spent a year in Osceola County, Florida. She had been living in Puerto Rico for six years when Hurricane Maria hit. A week after arriving in Florida, Then Ortiz moved into the Baymont Inn in Kissimmee, where she's been living ever since.

I came to Florida with my husband and my daughter. She bought the tickets, and we left through Ponce, but she returned to the island after a month. She is an English teacher. About a month after the hurricane she told us, "You are better off over there." I had lived in Osceola for a year once before, and

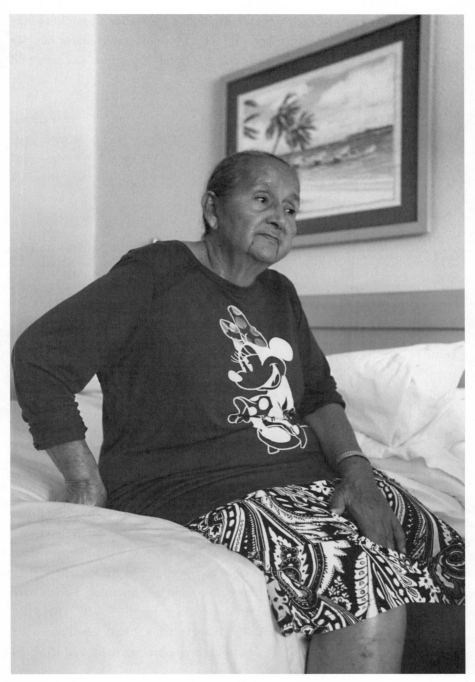

Rosa Then Ortiz

when I came we stayed with a friend for about a week. But we couldn't stay with her for long because my friend said the apartment would charge her. My daughter started looking until she found this hotel. She called, and they told her we were eligible to stay here. They even gave her a room until she left for the island.

Hurricane Irma was not as big a shock as Maria, which was more furious. For Maria a church friend told us, "You can't stay in your house with your husband." So we went to her house. I was secure in my neighbor's house, but I would glance out the window and could see the storm was very strong. I stayed with my neighbor for two weeks, and when I returned to my house for the first time it was so ugly. The winds entered the porch and destroyed two rooms. It made a big hole in each room. The ceiling panels became warped, and a lot of water entered. It looked like a river. My neighbor's house was fine because hers is made of cement, which is different from mine, which is made of wood and zinc. My house is very old, but, thank God, I only had the two holes in damages.

FEMA came to my house to investigate, but I told them I had to leave, to come to Florida, because of my husband's health condition. I waited three months to leave. A lot of help arrived in Guánica: The National Guard brought food and water, and the mayor also supplied food. A lot of things arrived from New York, from here in Orlando, and many other places. And they continue to help, I think, with the housing, sending construction material. My neighbor would take me to get supplies in town—I live about ten minutes from town. The people who worked at city hall helped out at the hospital. I went to the museum in the town plaza, which offered lunch every day at noon. It was already cooked for you. Oh, how I love my country. I'm grateful to God that we are alive, but my biggest worry was my husband. He fell down two times in the neighbor's house. I'm not sure what happened, but the bed was close to the floor, and I think he sat too close to the edge and fell off. He doesn't have enough strength to support himself. I couldn't do anything. I don't have much strength myself. I'm old and tired. I'm older than he is—he is seventy-five—but I do everything for him. My struggle is big. I have cried because I didn't want to come to Florida. I had a housekeeper in Puerto Rico who helped me. But we came here because of his situation.

I don't know how long this process will take. I don't know if it will be two years or three years, but, oh, how I love my country. I'm homesick for my country. Guánica is a town made of friendships. Everybody helps each other. If somebody has to come with a hammer and nails to fix your window, they help one another. I'm grateful for everything, and I pray for everything. You just can't babble for the sake of babbling. You have to pray and be thankful for all that has been done. I'm very grateful. After the hurricane, my husband got worse emotionally, and his nerves were bad. Even now I have to give him anxiety pills because he gets very anxious. He has so many health problems; his health condition is very serious. We couldn't call anywhere. There was no telephone service, no water, no electricity. We had no access to anything. If you had a prescription, there was no insurance plan. That was the situation we were in. I paid forty-five dollars for medication for my husband. He needed it, but the pharmacy couldn't contact the insurance company for my benefits. Many people had to pay cash. It was a sad, serious, and tough situation.

I remember as a young girl my mother would talk to me about the strong hurricanes that passed through the island. She told me how it was. You get nervous. It's like going crazy, I tell you. My nerves were bad, and my husband was so sick. You get desperate. He's been sick for three years. He has sciatica, a pinched nerve, arthritis, and now he has a hernia. He needs an operation and look where we are. I'm waiting to hear when doctors can operate on him. He needs a hospital bed. Where is it? I don't know. He can get it through the medical plan, but where would I put it? He has problems standing up. He needs help with a lot of things. He doesn't even have a bottle to urinate in. I may need to buy one. I don't have transportation here, but my neighbor has helped me. She has a car, but the car broke down. A mechanic came, and I think the car is ready now. For some medical appointments they send transportation to pick us up. If my daughter were here, we would already have a place to stay because she can drive. She's coming back when school closes to help us, but she will leave for the island again. She's coming only to help get us settled. I told her to take it easy. I applied for an apartment for the elderly in Winter Haven that a friend told me about. I was number 136 on the list, but now I am number 12, and I hope the number keeps going down. The complex has everything I need: internet, doctor, a social worker. It has a lot of possibilities. When we first arrived, I told my daughter, "Let's see if we can find an apartment." I want to be in a place where I can pay month to month. I don't want to sign a contract where I could lose out. You know the situation that's happening now? All the rents are going up. Even the friend I stayed with said her rent went up by one hundred dollars, although not because of us. That's what landlords are doing.

We're obligated to leave this hotel, but if I'm going to be on the street, I'd rather return to Puerto Rico. I tell you, I'm not going to live on the street. It was easier in Guánica because I have my own house, and nobody is going to throw me out because I own it. I have a car over there, too. People sometimes underestimate the value of a tropical country. If you don't have gas to cook, you look for charcoal. If you don't have electricity, you use candles. If you don't have running water, you can find water somewhere. In my house I have plantains, bananas, avocados, pomegranates. The avocados were so good. I tell you, I am *boricua* from head to toe.

But I tell you the truth, I can't complain in the sense that I have a roof over my head. They give you breakfast here: pancakes, juice, coffee. I feel fine. I have a lot of neighbors looking after me here. After the hurricane this place was full. It's still full, but some people have begun to leave. FEMA pays about one hundred dollars a day, but I'm not sure; the amount could be higher. I'm concerned for the children at the hotel. There was one upstairs who was very nervous. I could tell that many of the kids felt bad. One mother told me that after the hurricane she saw a change in her children. They had changed emotionally. She was taking them to counseling and social workers, but she has moved away.

I don't know how long I'm going to be here. I hope to return to Puerto Rico but not now, maybe in two years. I can't say bad things have happened to us because the hurricane happened due to nature. Storms and hurricanes are part of nature. It's something that had to happen. God is big and powerful. He has given me three revelations in my sleep in this bed. In the last one I was in the back part of my house, and a neighbor said, "Come and tell me what needs to be done in your patio." In the second dream I had two suitcases open on the floor, and I was looking for my plane tickets. I finally found them, and my husband was leaving with me. The first dream was about a plane leaving at 11:30, and I had to hurry to make the flight. We have faith and confidence in God and, God willing, everything will go well for us.

Wilda Cirino

I am here because of my son.

*Wilda Cirino, thirty-six, is from Loíza, Puerto Rico, but she fled to
Orlando with her infant son, Lionel, after Hurricane Maria, which
she said she spent with a friend near Hato Rey, in the San Juan area,
thinking things would be somewhat better than in Loíza. Cirino
had lived in Orlando for two years prior to Maria, from 2015 to 2017,
returning to Puerto Rico in the spring of 2017 to give birth to her child,
who was thirteen months old at the time of our interview. Fearing that
her son was becoming ill in Puerto Rico, she returned to the Orlando
area in November 2017 and had been staying four months at the
Baymont Inn in Kissimmee. Cirino took great pride in her room and
hospitality, placing a bouquet of yellow roses and daisies in a hospital
water jug on a table and offering coffee and flan, although she herself
had little.*

Right now I am a housewife taking care of my son, but I'm looking for a job
because I'm a hardworking person. I didn't prepare to be a single mother, but,
well, I'm not the first nor the last who hasn't prepared for this. In 2017 I left
Orlando for Puerto Rico because I found myself alone having my first child. I
needed the help of my family and decided to return to Loíza, to live with my
parents. The apartment where I had been staying in Orlando was jeopardizing my son's health. I asked the apartment managers for a change in apartment, but they weren't very flexible. The air-conditioning was not working,
and there was a situation with the bathtub that I hadn't noticed earlier. As
a responsible mother, for the love of my son and to keep from being alone, I
returned to Puerto Rico in April 2017. I lived with my parents, and then I went
to my grandmother's house. May she rest in peace.

I spent Hurricane Irma with my parents in Loíza. We came out all right,
although we had no electricity. There's always a problem with that little corner of Loíza. We are connected through Río Grande, and the electricity is

Wilda Cirino

always a little late in coming to our spot. We enjoyed the electricity for a couple of days until Maria came. When they announced the hurricane was coming, I decided to go with a friend who lived in San Juan and who opened her doors to me, because I was afraid of Maria, which was heading our way with more velocity. They said the sea would rise and flood the area. I spent a month and fifteen days with my friend. It was tough. There was no electricity. We had to walk distances to get money at the ATM. We had to do this practically every day in order to survive because we had very little left. It was very rough. I didn't plan well because I thought I would spend only three days with my friend. I took one formula for my son because he drank only special milk. When that milk ended, we used another type of milk. She gave me 1 percent fat milk and said, "Don't worry. This won't hurt him until he begins to adapt." I suffered a lot for my son because I knew he was being adversely affected due to the milk situation. But God was always there for us. He didn't leave us alone. He gave me strength and fortitude. I spent the time away from my family, and my son was able to survive it. About mid-October I returned to my parents' house in Loíza, helping them look for water and ice. I had left my family in good shape before heading to San Juan. We bought a generator, and I had brought sandbags to keep the water from entering through the bottom of the doors. We took measures to prevent things from getting worse. I hadn't counted on staying so long with my friend, but these things happen. Thank God our house in Loíza is made of cement with a cement roof too. We didn't have too many complications. Very little water got in the house, thank God, and everyone was fine. But we continued without electricity, and it was hot for my son, who by then was five or six months old. Everybody in our *barrio* had a generator, and the smell was making my son sick. He had a cough, and I took him to the emergency room because I noticed his chest was tightening. I concluded it was the gas fumes because there were a lot of generators around us. The noise was horrible. During the day it's okay, but when night arrived you slept very little because of the noise. Thank God that my parents' house has screens to protect us from the mosquitoes, which were also a threat.

I had a little money from my tax returns, and with that little bit of money I bought the ticket to Orlando. I didn't leave earlier because my son's medical appointments delayed us, so I ended up leaving on November 19, coming directly to Orlando after a very good friend opened her doors to me. I was with her three weeks; then FEMA gave me the opportunity to stay in a hotel, but it was only for a very short time, about six days. That was not convenient as I have such a young child, and I can't be up and down with him. That's not good for him or for me. Thank God I have transportation, a little car that I left in storage, thinking if things go well in Puerto Rico then I'll just sell the car. And if not, then I have a way of moving around if I have to return. My friend heard that in Kissimmee the hotel stay was much longer. I have been in this hotel since the end of December with my son, thank God. I don't have to go anywhere else, and I don't have problems with anyone. The hotel owners don't have any problems with me. I am a clean and orderly person. As you can see, I have order. My son is a good boy, and I love him above all else. He is my strength and my reason for being; that's why I'm here, because of him. I have been in Orlando four months, and everything has gone well. I've never been denied help when I asked for WIC [Women and Infant Care] or anything else. I've been searching for day care, but they tell me I'm not working, and I have to do this and I have to do that. They put a lot of obstacles in my way. Without day care I cannot go to work. There are rules, and then there are rules. There are rules that are too exaggerated. It's super-inconvenient for somebody like me who has always worked to be without a job because I can't generate income. I've looked into other strategies, and my parents and friends have always lent a hand, and for that I'm grateful. I'm also appreciative of the good people that God has placed in my path, but it hasn't been easy. Rents are very high. We should collect signatures to force rents to go down. But thank God that we are under this roof. FEMA has been good to us; I can't say it hasn't been. I'm very grateful for their help and the deadline extensions they have given us.

I always have a plan B and a plan C because you have to live with a plan. Before FEMA gave us an extension [for housing vouchers to June 30, 2018] I had contacted a friend, saying I didn't know how long the doors would be open for me here, and she invited me to her place. When FEMA granted the extension, I called her back and thanked her with all my heart for being willing to help. I am not on the street, thank God. If I can't live in this state, then I'll go to another. I have friends in Houston, another friend in Pennsylvania, and also a friend in Syracuse. I have friends, you see, and I always have a plan B or plan C because I have a child who depends on me, and I'm not going to permit anything to happen to him. If I'm okay, then he's okay. My plan is to keep fighting. I'm going to see apartments and continue pushing forward. I have plans to study, to take computer classes to improve my knowledge, and to continue improving my English. I speak a little English, and that's how I've survived. I like helping people so I'd like to do customer service. I'm going to continue pushing for childcare with 4C.* That's the kind of person I've always been. I'm not perfect, but I'm a good person and, even through all these experiences, there's always a good vibe, a positive vibe, a happy vibe. I've always said that with God everything is possible and without Him nothing is possible. He has a purpose for each of us. I experienced a pregnancy, my first, all

---

* 4C is a nonprofit organization based in Orange County, Florida, that helps parents with child-care resources and referrals, school readiness, voluntary pre-K, and early Head Start.

alone, and I can tell you that God was always with me. I had a beautiful natural childbirth with just a little pain. My friend cut the umbilical cord, and my son was born beautiful, and everything changed. I didn't fall into depression, and you know why? Because God is always in control. I have no resentment toward my son's father who disappeared, although I am disillusioned. I always pray to God to take care of him and protect him wherever he may be because in this little heart I have no hate. That seed is not in me.

I have looked for jobs through CareerSource and Manpower, and they've helped me a lot. I recommend them to others. I went to the Methodist church to ask for help, and I have a good caseworker. There is help out there—you just have to find it. It's not easy, but it's also not difficult. A lot of people feel inhibited because they don't speak English well, but that's false. If you're here, it's because you came with the mentality to forge ahead, not to limit yourself. I've always said that the problem with *boricuas* is that they have become accustomed to what's convenient. If you work, the government takes away aid, but if you're not working, it says, "I'll give you this aid." We have learned to lean on this. But when you come to a place like this, you have to work and work very hard because here you have to pay for everything. You can't think that you can be like you were in Puerto Rico. You must work here. It doesn't look good to be always asking and asking for things. You have to hit delete on that way of thinking because you can't live here the way you do in Puerto Rico. You have to think about nurturing yourself and protecting yourself. There is work, even if it's cleaning or sweeping up. When I was here in 2015 I worked in a hotel cleaning, and I also worked in fast food. I've done a little bit of everything. I want to do something different, so I'm looking for customer service work. I'm the type of person who learns fast, and I love to learn and to teach. I'm always open to new things. I'd like to take some seminars to become an event planner, or I'd like to work for myself. I like business. To work for other people is not easy. I have a lot of initiative, and the difference between here and my country is that when you have initiative here it's not acknowledged, but in Puerto Rico people love it. They like that you have initiative. I was in a situation where I said, "Wow, I have to adapt to this rhythm." It's like they ask you to do something, and that's all they want you to do. If I see that something else can be done, then I do it, and I say, "Hey, I did this, and let's work as a team." Your boss says, "You didn't have to do that." When I get that kind of response I have to adapt to the change. I try to limit myself a little to avoid problems and a certain rejection. That's why I've even thought of working for Uber because I can be my own boss, and I can be more responsive to my son. This is also the time for elections, and I'm considering a part-time job because I can spend more time with my son. I'd like to spend as much time with him as possible until he begins school.

A year from now I want a permanent roof for me and my son; I'd like to have a business. I'm passionate about everything, and I like coming up with ideas, and I want to share my ideas. I would like to feel that I have more direction. In life you have to be ready for everything, good and bad. You have to live in the present and have your head on right. You have to be connected with God. Believe me, if I weren't connected with God with all the things I've experienced that have brought tears to my eyes—I unload when I cry—but I am re-strengthened. I am not weakened. When you are with God, nothing weakens you. I am here, and I haven't surrendered. I tell people, "Don't surrender, continue fighting, prepare yourselves and find help because there is help in the libraries, in the churches. Don't feel alone but turn to God. With God you don't feel alone and you don't feel sad. There's life, there's light, and there's direction." I have cried and raised myself up again, and I'm reborn. I haven't become desperate, and I'm not going to leave my son with just anyone. He didn't ask to be born. I don't feel that he's a burden; he is my responsibility, and that's why I look out for what's best for him. I have enjoyed my time with my son a lot. He is super-happy and beautiful. He is my angel, and we have been a team since he was born.

Puerto Rico will always be my Puerto Rico. I could be anywhere, and my country is my country. I miss my family because my family, good or bad, is my family, and they have helped me, lent me a hand when I needed it. Everywhere I go I say, "I'm Puerto Rican, I'm from Loíza," whether people like it or not. Realistically, though, I'm better off here or in another state because I need the stability for me and my son. Everything I'm doing is for us two. If I return to Puerto Rico, my parents would help me, but what about a job? I would be in the same routine as before. Puerto Rico's minimum wage is $7.25 an hour. Who can live on $7.25 an hour? I did it for a while, and it's like living check to check. I'm not going to rest as long as God gives me spirit.

Miriam Echevarría and José Antonio Vázquez

Nobody can prepare for a hurricane like Maria.

Miriam Echevarría, forty-four years old, and husband, José Antonio Vázquez, forty-four, are from Barrio San José, in Toa Baja, Puerto Rico, one of the worst-hit towns during the hurricane due to flooding. She was a home health aide who cared for the elderly and sold homemade pastry on the side, while Vázquez worked as a security guard. The storm not only uprooted their home, which belonged to Vázquez's grandparents, but also caused significant mental and emotional upheaval for the couple, who were living at the Baymont Inn in Kissimmee at the time of this interview. They took a circular route to Florida, flying first to Texas, where a daughter lived, before landing in Orlando. They felt stymied, each wanting to move in a different direction, causing tension in the marriage.

[Miriam:] Irma was a regular storm for us. Yes, we had leaks, but it was not as grave as Hurricane Maria, which caused us more losses.

[José:] Nobody can prepare for a hurricane like Maria. You can have two or three weeks' worth of water, but that would not have been enough. Imagine, seven months later there is still no water or electricity. The lines for water and gas were kilometers long. There were little supermarkets open here and there, but they didn't have supplies. You would go to the supermarket with empty hands, and you'd return with empty hands. We had to stand in line two or three hours for two little bags of ice because they didn't give you more than that.

[Miriam:] On the night of the hurricane José had been recently operated on for a disc replacement. My mother-in-law also was with us, and she can hardly walk, has a heart condition, had a hip replacement and a shoulder replacement. She had a fractured rib, and all of that made things difficult for me because I was the one who had to care for them, bathe them, do everything for them. I asked my sister-in-law for help, to take her because her house was larger and more secure. I collected water and asked others to help me sweep leaves and help store or tie down other things around the house that might be dangerous—washer, dryer, windows—everything you were supposed to do to prepare and then wait.

[José:] We put up industrial zinc planks over the glass patio doors, but we left a one-inch opening between the planks to look out. We could see how parts of houses flew away. After all of this, I learned that you cannot play with nature.

[Miriam:] Toa Baja was one of the towns that suffered the most. We saw everything blow apart—planks of zinc, wood, wrought iron. Two nearby homes were already underwater. You could see only a little bit of a roof on a one-story house, and a two-story house with a second floor made of wood blew away. My neighbors knew we had the one-inch lookout, and they began to signal to us to get out, that the water may flood where we were, but thank God the water didn't reach us. I was afraid because I could run but José couldn't, and I feared that we would have to cross to our neighbor's home as the zinc and wood flew all around us. We did cross little by little, and it was astonishing to see the garbage, pieces of houses, and other material tossed around. I was desperate because I had to leave my two dogs behind. My husband said, "If you see the water pass this mark, then you know it will flood the house as well." It was horrible. All of us whose homes were flooding had to evacuate to my neighbor's house. My neighbor tried to get people out, and we helped out others who were stranded in their homes. The elderly people were crying because they lost everything. Their nerves were agitated, and they had left their medication behind.

A tree fell on our home, cracking apart the cement walls. Everything we owned got wet. I opened the door to the house and saw all the damage—my mother-in-law's mattress was destroyed—but the house itself didn't flood. Before the hurricane others had recommended that we go to a shelter, but we said no. The water had never risen to that level before. We didn't think it was going to be so strong a hurricane. My father-in-law encouraged us to go to my other sister-in-law's home. But we didn't want to bother anyone. We wanted to stay independent, plus we had our dogs. So we decided to stay, and thank God nothing happened to us. I had never lived through something like that, but compared with other people we were fine. After the hurricane the real struggle began. We had to get my mother-in-law; we had to find water and food. The National Guard soldiers who passed didn't understand Spanish.

Miriam Echevarría and José Antonio Vázquez

I know a little English, and people would call me: "Miriam, come here. Tell them I need a tarp." It was very difficult because at times the food and water were not enough. We would signal to one another when help arrived because sometimes they parked in one place, and neighbors who were farther up in the *parcelas** wouldn't have known about it. When we saw a truck coming and the soldiers said they were going to distribute goods, we all would run to the trucks without even knowing what they were going to distribute.

[José:] We never got help from the mayor of Toa Baja.[2] I think the river washed him away! The hurricane was in September, we left in January, and we never saw the mayor, at least not in Barrio San José.

[Miriam:] There was a guy who, God bless him wherever he is because we never saw him again, said, "Follow me. I'm going to distribute something." I went with a neighbor, and he had a truck full of bed comforters that were water-damaged. He said, "Leave them in the plastic bags in the sun and they will dry." Many of the comforters had bleached water lines where they were folded. He was giving them away six to a person or whatever you could grab. He asked me and my neighbor to help him distribute the comforters. People were asking for specific sizes. You couldn't ask for sizes! You had to take what you could get! He distributed what was left in the truck to people who hadn't taken any, leaving each with two or three comforters.

[José:] We stayed in Puerto Rico until January, but we had to leave the island because of my health conditions and because of my mother. She is the only one who takes care of us. She's the only person we have. FEMA said the house was dangerous because the tree that fell split our roof. We had to leave. When we left we first went to Texas.

[Miriam:] I lived many years in San Antonio, raising my two children there. José had never left Puerto Rico, and it took time to convince him to leave. I said, "Look at the conditions here and the situation with our medications." He had been hospitalized twice. I want to be clear; at that moment I just wanted to leave that hell. It was me alone against everything. Everything was negative instead of positive. I had to take care of him, his mental problems, the water and electric issues. I felt so alone and so bad

---

* *Parcelas* are small plots of land, usually located in rural areas, that the Puerto Rico government deeds over to low-income families to build homes.

that I said, "Let's get out of here or each of us is going to go crazy." I spoke with my daughter and we arrived in San Antonio, staying at a hotel. It didn't go too well for us because my daughter, who is only twenty-one years old, could help but only so much. The hotel was not like here, where you can walk to buy food. We were there one month, spending the little money we had on food, Uber, and crying, depressed—the same as in Puerto Rico but more alone because we hardly talked to anyone. So, we made the decision to return to Puerto Rico. That same day I called my nieces to buy the airline tickets, but his brother called and said their mother was in the hospital in serious condition. She was dying, and the doctor said those who were far away and wanted to see her should come. We made the decision to leave San Antonio and jump here because she was in Orlando. Her daughter couldn't handle her because she works and has children. I said, "I can't either because I'm with him, and he needs help too. She needs help; she is your mother." His mother primarily has a heart condition and can hardly walk. Not too long ago she had fluids in her lungs. I didn't want to come here because it represented yet another change. Before I left Texas, I had to go to the hospital because my blood pressure was very high. They forced me to go to the hospital because I didn't want to go.

[José:] Her blood pressure was 224.

[Miriam:] Still, I decided to support my husband and came to Orlando. I left the hospital at three in the morning, and by three in the afternoon I had to be on a flight. I arrived here crazy for some sleep because of the stress, and thinking my brother-in-law was going to help us. I saw my mother-in-law, and she was fine. It has been very difficult for us. We were in my brother-in-law's house in Kissimmee for two weeks. I thought that I could look for help in that time. I had heard there was a lot of help here at the airport and other places. I told him, "If you take me to these places I won't have to depend on you." There were eleven people in his house: children, nieces, and nephews. They didn't come from Puerto Rico; they all live in Orlando. He didn't take us to do anything.

[José:] They didn't take us to see not one apartment.

[Miriam:] I didn't like certain things I saw and knew I had to get out of there or explode, or they were going to have to call the police on me, or I was going to go crazy. I have to do something. I needed my space. I didn't know what to do, where to go. I have no car. Thank God my husband's aunt helped us find this place. She has been like an angel to us. She said it would have been better for us to stay with her and help take care of the mother, but I said no. I didn't come here to take care of her. I came here only to help. I am taking care of José. I have to take care of myself. I'm not emotionally well because I feel as if I'm in limbo. I have no way out. I want to go to work, but I can't work because I don't have a car. His emotional state is poor, and lately he is saying he doesn't want to live anymore, that he's going to throw himself from the balcony. He wants to go to Puerto Rico and leave me because he knows I'm not well. I take care of everyone with love, but there are moments I ask myself, "When are we going to get out of this?" Recently, we were in an uncertain situation, not knowing what was going to happen with the hotel vouchers, not having a place to go. Every day is the same: What's going to happen? We have knocked on a lot of doors to get help and haven't accomplished anything. Everything is negative. At times I say, "Let's return to Puerto Rico and see what we can do there," but things are so difficult there. It's like returning to the same thing we left behind. I wish there was help here so I could get a job, look for a place to live. Right now, he has no medical insurance, and he was referred to SSI,* but that is a long process. He visited a doctor who can help him with SSI, and now we have to wait. But time is what we don't have. Our time at the hotel is running out. I came here with FEMA money that paid for some of our losses in Puerto Rico. But we spend a lot of money here. The only thing I have left is $1,100 to rent an apartment. I called FEMA to ask if they could guarantee me a place to stay if I return to Puerto Rico, and they answered that our home had water and electricity.

[José:] The question I ask is, "For how many hours is there water and electricity?" How could they tell us that after they said we had to leave the house because it was uninhabitable? Second, the house is not ours; it belonged to my grandparents. But our plan is to return to Puerto Rico because we're not going to live on the streets here.

[Miriam:] We have tried looking for an apartment but they all tell us the same thing: we need three months' rent, and we have to earn three times the

---

* Supplemental Social Security income under which recipients, mostly poor, may qualify for Medicaid.

apartment rental cost. They ask for a deposit, and then they put you on a waiting list because they have no apartment to rent. The waiting list is long, and it could be more money we end up losing. I am not working, and he is not working, and I cannot live on my mother-in-law's Social Security income, which she offered to us. I cannot do that. I need to work, and even if I worked, the income wouldn't stretch that far. We have checked other hotels that might be cheaper. But even so, there would go the money we have saved for rent and we would wind up on the street when the money finishes. Everything is an obstacle. You try to move forward and hit upon another rock.

I have my own conditions and have not been able to see a doctor. I have anemia, for instance, and a thyroid condition. My sugar level is high, and my blood pressure went up. I went to a hospital here, but they wouldn't admit me; instead, they gave me a prescription. My state of energy and headaches affect me, but I push that all aside and continue to deal with him and my mother-in-law. But it's not easy. I'm not well mentally. I hardly sleep. I try not to think of these things, but my thoughts automatically turn to what am I going to do. Where can I look for help? Where can I call? This is strong stuff.

[José:] You feel like throwing in the towel. I have a pain that I cannot support. I can barely withstand the pain in my legs. I cannot take physical therapy because once they gave me therapy, and I couldn't walk for days. It was suspended because supposedly the circulation in my legs is clogged. So, my health suffers from circulation and back problems. We have no medical insurance to pay for treatment for her or me. Even before leaving Puerto Rico our medical care was falling apart after services were suspended, but here it has become worse. We went to a clinic, and they said you have to obtain medical insurance first before you can find a specialist.

[Miriam:] This has been a lesson. We saw people who became more united—family, neighbors, people who didn't talk to each other for years. But I also saw many horrible things. How can somebody deny food and water to others, fight in supermarkets for things they could divide among themselves? If it had been me, I would have said, "There's only one case of water left. Let's split the cost and divide it. You take half and I take half." Not everyone thinks that way. There were people who the more they had, the more they wanted. That's why I cling to God a lot.

Sugeilly Meléndez and Layla Martínez Meléndez

Sugeilly Meléndez and Layla Martínez Meléndez

I was no longer "la loca" because I was prepared.

Sugeilly Meléndez of Cidra, Puerto Rico, is thirty-three years old and has an eight-year-old daughter, Layla Zoe Martínez Meléndez. She arrived in Florida in December 2017, taking up immediate residence at the Baymont Inn in Kissimmee. Meléndez was an elderly care worker in Puerto Rico, and perhaps that's a reason she developed a close relationship with Rosa Then Ortiz and her husband, Cruz Then Lorenzo, an elderly couple also staying at the hotel whose interview appears in this chapter. She is one of the few evacuees who planned to return to Puerto Rico, saying her options were limited in Florida. However, she left the door open to returning to Florida in the future.

I had an apartment in Cidra across the street from my grandmother's house because I wanted to be close to her since she raised me. My grandmother died much before the hurricane, and an aunt plus other family members lived in her house. After she died, I had thought of moving away, but I didn't. When the hurricane came, I sought refuge in another aunt's home because all the houses in her area were made of cement. I thought the hurricane wasn't going to be that strong. But at one point I thought the house was going to blow away, pulled up from the roots, because it shook at the same time. I heard the storm shutters as they were yanked out, and I thought, there goes one shutter, and there goes another shutter. I saw the trees come to rest on the windows of my aunt's house. I was going to break one of my aunt's windows to see if I could fit through there, but I couldn't. Still, I didn't think the damage would be that great, but when it came time to leave, I couldn't because there were trees and electric poles strewn all over the streets. My daughter's dad traveled from Bayamóncito to Cidra on foot with a machete to make sure his daughter was okay.

After two days some of the electric posts were removed and I went out and said to myself, "But what is this?" Some streets had collapsed, and when I got to my house the roof was gone. It had blown away, and I started to cry because, imagine, where am I going to live? The door was blown into the house, and I didn't know where my things were—the television, my daughter's doll collection. Everything was gone, things that I owned for years vanished in one night. When people finally came out of their homes, they were hungry because they had nothing to eat. Thank God that I have always stored a lot of food. I've always said that you have to be prepared because you don't know what's coming. You have to have a first aid kit and a bag with all of your documents. I've always had that. When there was no food, I had cases of canned sausages, cases of canned corned beef, cases of canned vegetables, cases of water—so much so that they called me "la loca." My uncle was going crazy because he had no water, but I was the only one who had water—me, "la loca." I was no longer "la loca" because I was prepared. You always have to have food stored away for situations like this. I returned to my aunt's house but was able to stay only two or three months because she couldn't withstand the depression she felt, plus she had a pending trip, so I had to go to another aunt's whose house was covered with a tarp.

My daughter suffers from pneumonia. She gets asthma, and after the hurricane she wasn't even getting asthma anymore. Her sickness would transition quickly from bronchitis to pneumonia. Within two weeks she had an asthma attack, but how was I going to give her therapy [with a nebulizer] if I had no electricity? She was hospitalized twice in Cayey. She had great pediatricians, who told me I had to be very careful with her. I ended up going to Bayamón, staying three days at a friend's place in public housing in order to get therapy for my daughter. I had a bag of her medication so I was okay on that end. I was told not to go to a hospital because the hospitals had no electricity. Thank God that in those three days she began to improve, but that's when I made the decision that I had to leave, more for her benefit than my own. I had two alternatives: my daughter dies or I leave. Her father, who is very strict and didn't want her to travel, agreed for us to leave. We signed legal papers allowing me to travel with her, and I brought her here. Plus, people were taking advantage of the situation in Puerto Rico after the hurricane, raising rents. One room would cost $400. What is that? The rent was $300 or $350 before. Everything went up. If you wanted a generator, you had to pay triple the normal price.

I didn't know much about Florida but I had friends who said they were coming here so I said, "Well, I'm going too." I had never been here. I worked so I had a little bit of savings. When I got here in December a person related to my mother's stepfather was waiting for me, and they brought me directly to this hotel. I had everything planned out. I had called to make the reservation, but I became depressed because I didn't know anyone and I didn't dare go out. People started putting things in my head, like be careful of the sexual predators. As a single mother I was afraid, but not anymore. Now I go everywhere. The people here at the hotel helped me. They said, "No, you can't stay indoors, you have to go out." I would go out and take the bus but always with another person, not alone with my daughter. I had a situation at a bus terminal where a man was looking a lot at my daughter. Everyone said that I really had to hold onto my daughter because anybody could grab her. A month after I arrived a cousin gave me a car to help me out. If my daughter gets sick, I have to be able to take her to a hospital, and she's already had two asthma attacks.

FEMA told me that there would be more hotels and more opportunity to rent an apartment. They said I would have four months in a hotel. But a single person cannot make it. It has to be more than one person. You need to have two jobs, and I can't leave my daughter alone for long periods of time. When she started school she was bullied. They said they were going to kill her, which traumatized her. The teachers didn't deal well with the situation, and I had to take her out of school. My daughter said she preferred to be institutionalized than return to school because the bullying was tough. She's been out of school for two months, but I plan to return to Puerto Rico. The government denied me all help. My food stamps were fifteen dollars, and I can't survive on that. There was another person at the hotel who also was awarded only fifteen dollars in food stamps. They have denied me so many things that I am preparing to leave. They said I was the target of identity theft. I don't have enough documentation, so they have closed the doors to me. A sister who lives in New York said that shouldn't have happened because I have a daughter who's a minor. Plus, they know that I'm working on this. There is a lawsuit. I can't deal with all this.

I was working at a Disney property four hours a day to provide food for my daughter. A friend, one of many I have made here, would take care of my daughter while I worked. We help each other here. My neighbors are always watching out for me and my daughter. A neighbor might say, "I have rice with codfish." Another neighbor offered me a small grocery purchase. People help each other. Thank God that I haven't lacked for that. I try to help, too, because there are people who don't have anyone helping them. I am helping the elderly couple downstairs. When her husband gets sick, I am the one who tries to help, taking them to doctors. She says, "You are like my daughter." If I see that people need help, especially the elderly, I try to help. You have to give in order to receive, but it's better to give, and I always receive. I left my job about two weeks ago because I plan to leave. I don't have a date certain for leaving because I'm waiting for my last paycheck. I don't feel secure here. You have to be better prepared to come here. It's better to have a secure job and rent an apartment before leaving Puerto Rico. I plan to return to Puerto Rico for a year. A church brigade is going to repair my property, but in order for that to happen I have to be there. I had to put myself on a waiting list. I regret now not moving earlier from that house to a cement house, as I had wanted. I have regretted it a thousand times. I plan to stay in a hotel in Puerto Rico, but if that doesn't work out, I'll stay with a friend who has opened the doors of her home to me. I would like to rent a home that has electricity because in Puerto Rico the light comes and goes, comes and goes. The electricity is not so much for the air-conditioning but for the refrigerator and to be able to give my daughter her therapy.

I don't know how long the repairs will take, but once that's completed, I plan to return to Florida for good. I like it here. It's different. My family has told me to stay out here, but right now my brother is in prison, and I want to see him. I want to know why he's in prison. I went through some bad experiences in Florida, but now I have an idea of how this place is. I didn't know, for instance, that renting a house or apartment takes time. Now I have an idea of how to fill out applications for rentals and low-income housing. I search the internet for information, and if I leave Puerto Rico again, I will have my housing secured and a job waiting. I learned that you cannot do things all crazy. You have to have money, good savings, and arrive here knowing where you are going to stay and, of course, have a good job. You should bring at least ten thousand dollars in order to survive. Don't do things the crazy way. Florida is not a world of magic and wonder. It's very tough. When you arrive, you find out that things are different, you have to work hard.

Layla Martínez Meléndez,
eight years old, daughter:

I was sleeping during the hurricane, but I wasn't afraid. There was no reason to be afraid. When there was no light, I used the flashlight of the cell phone. My father came after the hurricane and after a while he left. The next day I saw that our home was destroyed; my mother was crying, and I told my mother not to cry. Then we came here. I didn't like the plane ride because it was boring. The only thing I liked about it was the window. I wanted to come here, but the school was bad. I received a lot of bullying in school because I didn't speak English. My *mamá* took me out. The thing I like most about Florida are the parks, but I want to return to Puerto Rico because I have friends there. I want to see my father when I get back, ride my new bicycle on the beach. My father said I could go gliding with him. I'm going to eat *churrasco* with French fries and a milk shake and a *bacalaíto*. I talk with my friends on the phone and tell them I will see them soon.

4

SETTLING IN

Rebecca Colón

I had a conversation with God.

Rebecca Colón, forty-two, originally from Río Piedras, Puerto Rico, had been living for about three years in Canóvanas's Loma sector, in Barrio Cubuy, to the east of San Juan. She and her husband had bought a nearly three-acre farm that came with an old cement house because they wanted to live in the country. They spent Hurricane Irma in Canóvanas but for Maria they went to the Carolina area, which is close to Canóvanas and where each has family members. Colón is a music teacher and her husband, Garibaldi Nevarez, forty-two, drove a tourist van in Puerto Rico. The family, including son Gari G. Nevarez, eleven, and daughter Andrea S. Nevarez, eight, had visited Pennsylvania, North Carolina, and Florida the summer before the hurricane, deciding that one day Florida might be a good place in which to relocate.

We bought a farm in Canóvanas that had an old, established house on it. We worked on the house until we were able to inhabit it. It's a house made of poured cement, and our neighbors tell us that many years ago coffee farmwork-

Rebecca Colón. Photograph by María T. Padilla.

ers used to live in it. A man once told me that he lived in the house when he was a young man, and at that time he was ninety-eight years old! Different owners throughout the years continued to add to the house, so that by the time we bought it, it had two bedrooms and a wraparound porch. We Puerto Ricans like to spend the hurricanes among family members, with fear but also together. My husband said, "Let's buy chocolate to make hot chocolate, and we'll spend the hurricane in the house." We wanted to live the first experience of a hurricane in the country, and that's what we did. We secured the house, put plywood over the windows on the inside. It was not a pleasant experience. In the first hours that Irma hit she took our electricity. In the middle of the hurricane, my husband and me had to place concrete blocks inside my old Pathfinder to weigh it down because it was dancing in the wind. We had put some blocks in it earlier in the afternoon, but this time we also used cords to tie the *guagua*, or van, to the columns of the porch. If we hadn't done that, the van would have blown away. By eight in the evening, for the first time in my life, I'm feeling the roof shake. I'm feeling stressed so I take some [Tylenol®] PM because my anxiety was high. That was going to be the only way I could get some sleep and get my kids to go to sleep. Remember, there is more noise in the countryside. When we woke up there was calm. We decided to go out in the community to see what had happened to our neighbors. We found that we lost the kids' trampoline. It had tumbled down the hill, its legs all bent. Many trees fell over. And from that point on we never regained electricity. I later found out it returned in May 2018. But nothing happened to the house. We were super-secure there. We never lost cell communication either, and I was able to talk with my sisters the next day. The Maria experience was not the same.

My father-in-law lives alone in Carolina, and we decided to be with him, leaving Canóvanas a few days before Maria. My husband and kids wanted to return to the house, but I wasn't so sure because I had already experienced a lot of anxiety. So I had a conversation with God. I prayed, "Please God, send me a sign so I can decide whether I'm going to stay up there or not." I thought about God a lot and said to myself, "You are going to send me that sign." The day arrives for Maria, and we head out from my father-in-law's house about noon, my husband in front in the Pathfinder and me with the kids in a new Toyota I bought after Irma. We are climbing curve after curve, to which we are accustomed, when suddenly a gigantic tree fell in front of my car, and I had to hit the brakes. It almost hit my bumper. My son became frightened. I drove slowly around the tree to get to my house because there's a thirty-foot cliff on the other side of the tree. That's when I thought, "Thank you, God. You gave me the sign I was waiting for." I had been waiting for the sign for a week, but I didn't tell anyone. "You tell me," I pleaded with God. "I will do what you say." I continued to the house, telling the kids to stay calm. "Don't be hysterical," I said, "because the calmer we are the better the decisions we can make." We continued on to the house, where my husband had already nailed plywood to the windows. He was in the last stages of preparing the house. I told my children that when we reached the house, they were to grab their suitcases and throw their clothes in. "Don't worry about folding the clothes," I said. "Just empty the drawers into the suitcases." I was in a rush, and those were my first instructions. "Don't ask me anything, don't tell me anything. Find your suitcases and just throw your clothes inside. That's what we're going to do." So when we arrived at the house I had already decided that we wouldn't pass Hurricane Maria there. My husband was a little shocked. He said, "How can that be? The tree is nothing." But I said, "This is what we're going to do." I tell you, our Pathfinder looked as if we had moved that day to the countryside. It was filled up to the top. I asked my husband to tie some things to the top. He complained every step of the way. "Why are you taking that?," he asked. I had toys, all my files, a generator we had bought for Irma. I had a sensation as if I were on automatic. I was determined to do what my heart said. Our house is the last one on the street. I worried it could tumble down the cliff in a landslide, although my father, who is a farmer, said we lived in a privileged area because our house was constructed on solid rock. "That's never going to go," he said. But the fallen tree told me what I had to do. So we left to my father-in-law's house in Carolina. We couldn't fit another item in the cars. We were pinned to our seats and could hardly move.

My father-in-law still lives in the home my husband grew up in, on the low end of a hilly street near the Río Grande de Loíza, a large river. But nobody had told us anything about the approaching storm. The governor's message was, "We don't know what can happen." We put the kids to sleep, but we didn't sleep at all that night. The hurricane arrived around three in the morning. I could see how it nearly toppled trees. It was frightening. There was no electricity. It was dark. We were standing in the dining room at one point when a neighbor ran out of his house crying, "Help!" as if it were coming out of his very soul. We quickly opened the door and he, his wife, two kids, and dogs entered. "Our house has flooded," he said. I thought, "Dear God, the river." We had to think quickly. I had made the decision to put my new car in that neighbor's carport because my father-in-law had no space in his, and the Pathfinder was parked outside. When I glanced outside, the whole street was filled with water, black water, brownish water. I thought, "The Río Grande de Loíza has reached us." It had rained a lot. I was thinking of my new car, but my husband said, "That's a material thing." I had done everything I could to save my things. I said, "Let's move the car out of the neighbor's carport." "My wife is crazy," he said, but he managed to get the car out of the carport, and we saved it. We parked it on the street because there was no other place for it.

I woke the kids, thinking that the river is coming and we have to leave. We needed to go higher up the hill. We may need to go from house to house up the hill if need be. We went to another neighbor's house, and there we stayed a while. It was horrible. The water continued to rise. Between five thirty and six in the morning we were back on the street asking for refuge. Five or six houses farther up, they opened the door to us. Several didn't open the door. Perhaps they didn't hear us. I don't know. My husband helped other older folks in the neighborhood get out of their homes. We were walking in water. I tried saving some things by placing them on top of the counters, hoping the water wouldn't reach that high. We took the suitcases and floated them on the water as we walked to higher ground. I had given my daughter a backpack to weigh her down, but I could see the wind pushing her as she walked along the sidewalk. I told my husband to go with her to keep her from flying away. The wind gave me an incredible shove, and I wound up three houses beyond the house we were going to. I couldn't stop. By the time we reached the last house we stayed at, I couldn't carry all these things anymore. I decided to open the Pathfinder and stuff my things in there. During the night I heard on a battery-operated radio that the river in Manatí had overflowed as never before, and my mother and grandmother live in Manatí near the Manataubón River.[*] I almost had to take a pill knowing they were so close to the river. The day before I had told my mom to use an inflatable mattress, thinking she could place my grandmother on the mattress and float. You never know what's going to happen. We were at the last house until eleven in the morning.

---

[*] The Manataubón River is popularly known as the Río Grande de Manatí.

We learned that it was not the Río Grande de Loíza that had risen but a sewage drain that had become covered with leaves and the black sewage water seeped out. It was very disagreeable. We returned to my father-in-law's house and began helping the community to clean up the drain opening so the water could drain into it. I could see that some cars that hadn't been moved from carports had water damage up to the top. That same day around five thirty in the afternoon I wanted to see what had happened to our country house. But before we reached our house, we went to Manatí to check on my mother. We took the toll road, and that turned out to be an odyssey. We had to get out of the car along with other people and cut trees to remove them from the road in order to keep going. At one point there was an immense traffic jam. We almost turned around, but a police patrol said the road would soon open. When we got to Manatí I saw the river near the Number 2,* but we couldn't get into the subdivision. I was worried about my mother. I had to see my mother. The guard said we couldn't enter because there may be live wires, but I had to see my mother. She lives with her brother, his wife, and my grandmother, and she's the only one in good health. He said we could enter only at our own risk, so that's what I did. I went on foot, jumping over and under trees until I got to the entrance. The Manataubón River had risen as high as the road. When I got to my mother, we both started crying because she never thought we'd reach her. I helped her with some things and stabilized her. But maybe I'm confusing the days because we brought her a gallon of gasoline for her generator, and there was a crisis of gasoline in the country. My husband and father-in-law would get up at three in the morning to get in line for gasoline without knowing if they'd be able to buy a little gasoline.

I was very concerned about the water because there was a moment when you couldn't find drinking water. I was very afraid, but I didn't verbalize it. When you're a mom and have minors depending on you, I thought, "Dear God, how am I going to feed my children?" Food was scarce. We ate a lot of chicken many days. Chicken, chicken, every day. I tried to vary the menu: I stewed it, I fried it, I tried to cook it all kinds of ways. There was nothing else. One day we found pork chops, and that was a feast. Otherwise, we ate a lot

---

* Puerto Rico's old main roads are numbered 1, 2, and 3. They were built along the coast, with the Number 1 along the southern coast, the Number 2 hugging the western coast, and the Number 3 traveling down the eastern coast.

of canned food: tuna, salmon, even canned chicken, which I had never seen before and was unable to eat it.

I saw my father every day. He is in his seventies and living with a childhood friend because, it just so happened, each separated from their wives about the same time. They share an apartment in Carolina. I would take them the canned chicken and say, "You two please eat this chicken!" I also took them water and rice. The town of Canóvanas and the mayor had given out food, including military rations. I didn't get any, but we did get canned food. Another issue was the inability to draw money from the ATM. When rumors hit that an ATM was functioning, the lines would be enormous. My husband had had the sixth sense to take out money from the ATM before the hurricane, and we stretched the cash until we were able to find an ATM to take out more money. My father-in-law also had a little money. It was a moment of unity. Never before had we been so united. On another occasion we collected drinking water in jugs and filled my husband's tourist van. We took the water to Humacao* because we had read an SOS on social media that they needed water. The whole family got into the van; we took musical instruments, and we sang *plena*,† giving out water from house to house in the pueblo. We took a case of water to each of our neighbors in the country. It was such a beautiful moment to grow and give each other a hand. We tried to do that with other people. Our portable generator gave light to our neighbors who plugged in their extension cords, and in this way they had a little light in the evenings.

At our country house, the hurricane swept and cleaned away so much greenery that we saw things on the mountainside that we had never seen before. I said, "Wow, that house was there? Wow, look at the river." When we reached near our street there were a lot of trees strewn across the path, so we left the car and walked on foot for about a mile, behind other houses, through the mud. The hurricane washed away a road, leaving the community unable to communicate. The *brea*, or pitch, had collapsed way down. It was incredible. It looked as if a meteorite had fallen and created a crater— boom!—separating us from the other side. The sign that God sent me was the best thing that could have happened to us because five families were left

---

* Humacao, a town on the east coast not far from Canóvanas, suffered major damages.

† *Plena* is a Puerto Rico music style known for its lyrics. It comes out of the *bomba* tradition, which evolved from the traditions of enslaved black Puerto Ricans in the seventeenth century.

without communication and were stuck inside their homes. It wasn't until April or May 2018 that the area returned to normal. Not able to reach our home, we returned to my father-in-law's house in Carolina. On our return, I was able to see our house up high, and I had never been able to see my house before because it had been hidden by trees. I could see that my house was OK. My father was right: the house withstood the worst. But we left without seeing the inside of the house.

I interviewed my neighbors afterward, and they said they felt the wind blowing at over 200 miles per hour. They had lived through Hugo and other hurricanes but never one like this. They heard loud gusts that went "zoom," and when they looked out the window they saw nothing. The wind had taken everything in one gust. I thought, "I would have died." If I had to take PM to sleep during Irma, I would have needed emergency assistance, and nobody would have been able to help me. Later, I told my husband, "See why we had to take our things?" I was able to enter the house days later. It was fine; only a little water had entered under a door. Even the washing machine and dryer that I had tied to a column on the porch were still there. But we couldn't stay because there was no electricity, no access by car. My family members created a human chain to help me take things out of the house—televisions and other things. People were breaking into homes, and I didn't want them to take my things.

The Department of Education gave instructions for teachers to report to their schools. When I went to my school in Juncos, I discovered that it had been destroyed. I ended up working at a neighborhood school in Carolina, helping parents and giving out lunches. We didn't hold classes. We spent our time engaged in arts and crafts to entertain the children because it had not been easy for them. We also spent the first day listening to the children's stories. Each one had a story. If I had survived a crisis, so had many other Puerto Ricans. There were children who couldn't leave the schools because their homes had been damaged or destroyed. The street filled with children playing, riding bicycles. Playing cards and dominoes became valuable items since we didn't have enough things to entertain us during evenings without electricity. We couldn't find enough things to entertain us. Just as the water would disappear, so would the playing cards. That's how we passed our days, waiting to see what would happen tomorrow. We lived like this for weeks and weeks.

Then I get a call from my husband's cousin in Winter Haven, asking us to come to Florida. She and her husband have four children and her father, a veteran, lives with them. We had never had a close relationship. We shared Christmas activities when they lived in Puerto Rico, but that was it. In my forty-two years I had never lived in another person's house. She has four children and I have two, and the thing I was most concerned about was their education. My son is an honor student, and my daughter is a good student, too. Two months had already passed, and there was no school in sight, no immediate or intermediate solution to the school situation. This was going to be indefinite. I thought of my children. We had just returned from Florida during the summer. We all fell in love with Florida. My son had a longing to live in Florida, and I thought, "Well, one day." But we had jobs in Puerto Rico; what are we going to do in Florida? When my husband's cousin called, I thought, "It must be that we're going to live in Florida as my son had wished." We had gotten to know our cousin better during the summer, and she had already looked into schools for the kids and teaching positions for me.

I wasn't sure if that was the right thing to do, but I decided I would come first to see what help was available, leaving my children with their father. I came on October 27, about a month after the hurricane. In Puerto Rico we had heard that there was help at the airport, that you go to the airport and all the help is there. I came through Fort Lauderdale, and they didn't have help at the airport. I spent the night at another cousin's house. The next day I took the Amtrak to Winter Haven by myself. It was divine, an experience I'll never forget. That same day we went to the Orlando airport, and just as they had said, there were representatives from Orange County and Osceola. I gave them copies of my teaching certificates, and they sent me links where I could apply for Florida teacher certification. I changed my driver's license to Florida at the airport, even though I still wasn't sure if I would stay. Some people had established a place in Kissimmee where you could get food, clothing, and anything else they had that you needed. It was all donated, and people had written messages on items, like "We are rooting for you." Tears sprang from my eyes. It was an intense moment. I never thought I would be an evacuee who needed help. Our cousin said to bring the children. "We'll find them schools," she said. My family arrived November 7, and I was anxious because I had never lived with anyone else. Then I found out that FEMA was handing out hotel vouchers, and I thought, "That's what I'm going to do." I would have my own space. We wouldn't be bothering anyone. You can hear everything in a house with Florida construction. Everything. The first place we went to was the Rose Motel in Winter Haven. School had already started, and it was nearby. I had asked the Puerto Rico Department of Education for an unpaid leave, and with the last check I received I bought a 2003 Honda Odyssey so I could move around. It was not a pretty hotel. It's old, and it had a strong smell. That first night my son complained, "Is this where we're going to live?" I said, "We're still living day to day. This is help the government has given us." After two nights, we moved to another hotel closer to Legoland. We didn't last two days there when I found another hotel closer to Lakeland. We stayed there three months until FEMA said the vouchers were going to end. My husband started working housekeeping in Disney World. In Puerto Rico he drove a tourist van, but over here we are starting from zero. Our cousin's husband works at Disney, and he said they take everyone, and that is a way to get started.

We still had some savings, and with that we bought another car, an Altima, for him. Otherwise, there is no way we can work and manage.

Disney interviewed my husband in January. I was not working. I wanted to make sure my kids were situated. I didn't understand the school buses. They pick you up so early in the morning, and it's still dark. Besides, it's now December so it's also cold. I wanted to understand how all this works, so we took food stamps until our plan took shape. I went to UPS, and they hired me, but I didn't go because they work Christmas Eve and Thanksgiving, and I couldn't burden our cousin, who had already done so much for us. I speak a little English, but my husband speaks it better. I knew I would have to work at a school so that our schedules would coincide, since I don't have anyone who can take care of our children. I applied in Osceola County as a paraprofessional, which is like a teacher's aide. The pay is not like a teacher's, but I'm in the classroom. I have seventeen years of experience, a master's degree, and in Puerto Rico I once was a school principal and worked at the school district level. I have a certificate for a school principal and also a certificate for music teacher. When I arrived here the people at the airport said, "Wow!" I went to a lot of schools and interviewed with principals. Here the principal hires you, but nobody hired me, as a para or anything else. I thought I probably have more experience than the principal looking at my résumé. So, I rewrote my résumé, eliminating seven years of experience and my master's degree. I went to Palmetto Elementary

School in Poinciana in late January, feeling down because I didn't think they would hire me. The principal spoke to me in English, but an English with an accent like Spanish-speakers have. I answered everything he asked me because I understood him so well. He accepted all my credentials. I was hired as a physical education aide. I was nervous, but I thought, "I'll be working with children." When I get there, the teacher is Puerto Rican too, from the town of San Sebastián. He helped me a lot. When the school year ended, the principal said he didn't want me as a para anymore. He wanted me as a teacher. Then I noticed that positions for music teacher opened up in a school near Palmetto. I applied, and I was hired. I still didn't know if we were going to stay. My husband, Gari, every day would ask: "We stay or we go? We stay or we go?" I still didn't know. That's when the path to Florida opened up. Many doors opened for me.

My husband found this apartment in April. He came to ask about an apartment and was told none were available. The person who tended him was Puerto Rican, and the next day we got a call about an available two-bedroom apartment. You have to earn a certain amount to live here, no more than $20,000-odd a year. We signed a contract. Our rent includes water. In Puerto Rico I lived in a beautiful countryside with a $175 monthly electric bill. When I got here the apartment office told me that I couldn't turn off the air-conditioning. I thought, "What?" She said things are different here. You have to leave the air-conditioning on at 75 degrees so as not to get mold. When the first electric bill came it was $98. Only $98 and at 75 degrees! How different you live here. I tell you, all the doors opened for us. For now, we will stay here. I want to work and find out how much I can earn because the school district accepted all my credentials. We still pay the mortgage on the house in Puerto Rico. Even though we don't live there, we didn't want to give up the house. FEMA went to look at the home, and the inspector said, "Wow, this is a paradise." We need to seal the roof to prevent leaks, and now we have a lot of rats. But for now, we will stay here. My son is attending a good charter school, and this year he made the honor roll. He's the one who knows English and helps me. My daughter will come with me to attend my school. She had more difficulty with English, but everything has gone super. I saw the classroom assigned to me, and I love it. There are a lot of Puerto Ricans here. About 75 percent of the teachers at the school are Puerto Rican.

I would like to bring my parents here, but my mother still cares for her mother, and it would be difficult to bring her because she is bedridden. My father is alone and I would like to bring him because of his health. The last time I saw him he seemed anxious. He has panic attacks. His blood pressure rises, and all of that is emotional. That would be our next priority. I would like to buy a house here, but I don't want to get overcome with debt. When I left Puerto Rico, I left it in crisis. I've been back two times, and the situation has improved. There's food in the supermarkets, and the banks are functioning. We listen to news of the island. I miss my family. But there is nothing to look for there yet. Things are worse. There's no future. Schools don't have the educational priority one would expect. It doesn't seem as if teachers are going to have pensions. In this sense, Puerto Rico has a long way to go. A lot of people never thought they would live through what they have lived through. In Puerto Rico we needed to gain some maturity about some things. The hurricane helped us grow as human beings. It helped me become a stronger person. It helped me to better appreciate life. Puerto Ricans needed to live through an experience like this in order to grow. I think that's the most important thing. Everything we have lived through we ought to carry it and overcome it. Look at all the doors that have opened up. We had to live through the hurricane to arrive at this moment.

Nydia L. Irizarry Ramírez

Dying is a big word for me.

Nydia L. Irizarry Ramírez, forty-five, of Manatí, Puerto Rico, arrived in Orlando on October 24, 2017, on a humanitarian flight with her two children, son Félix Rodríguez, eleven, and daughter Keishla Betancourt, twenty-three, who was diagnosed with Hodgkin's lymphoma at age seventeen. The flight was arranged by the American Cancer Society, which had airlifted cancer patients out of Puerto Rico with the help of sponsors and donors. She is now living in an apartment in Orlando working in a temporary job at an Episcopal church.

Nydia Irizarry Ramírez

We came after Maria because my daughter, who was twenty-two at the time, is a cancer patient, and we needed to get out of the island because services were awful. Everything was horrible after Maria, and her health condition was getting weaker, so we opted to come here. In Puerto Rico I lived in my parents' house in Manatí. My mother died in January 2017, and the three of us lived in the house. Irma scared us because we spent a week without electricity and water, but we recuperated quickly. For Maria we were more trusting than normal. We prepared as if it would be a light storm, but then things became very difficult. There were many hours of rain, wind, and destruction. We didn't stay in my house but with a friend of my daughter's whom I consider a son. He's a good guy and lives about five minutes away. He didn't think our house was secure enough and wanted us to stay with him so he could watch over us. He works in a hospital in Manatí, and if there had been an emergency with my daughter, he would have been able to call or take her to the hospital much faster. During the hurricane I became very anxious and desperate. I could hear the trees snapping and the sound of the wind. I could see the palm fronds falling and cisterns flying. It was total destruction. Water levels were higher than the pavement. I thought of my home because it has front glass windows, and I didn't have time to cover them. I feared the water would enter through the glass windows, and that's exactly what happened.

Water reached the bottom of the kitchen cabinets. It damaged my dining room and furniture. The water reached the hallway and into my daughter's room. A tornado passed through Manatí, and it was so strong that it yanked a window from the cement frame and flung it. Water came in as well. At the back of the house, the tornado ripped an aluminum awning and folded it as if with its hands. It tore off another window and threw it on the patio. The storm just came to destroy. There wasn't a tree that remained standing. I had fruit trees—three lemon trees and orchids that my mom cultivated. I had oregano and parsley plants. I have a mango tree that is over forty years old, and although it didn't snap, the storm managed to peel off its leaves. The storm couldn't handle the mango tree. All that the storm could take it did and left everything dry. The storm bent a light post on the street at the back of the house, and the wires fell on my house. They could have been live wires. That post was very old. All I could do was cry, cry, and cry until I was fatigued, but at the same time I thanked God because we were alive. If my mother had been alive, she would not have been able to withstand the destruction of the hurricane, but my mother departed before the hurricane. I tell you, once the storm started in Puerto Rico there was no way to contact paramedics. There were no ambulances; there was no police. No one was going to rescue anyone. I know that my mother would have died. The sound and the shock would have been enough. Our neighbors said the sound of the hurricane was horrible, ghostly, as if someone were talking. My daughter took a Xanax and remained tranquil. She slept during the hurricane. She didn't want to see anything. My son was the only one who saw everything; he was always with me. He was scared, listening to the storm, which like a hurricane had no pity.

The big issue after the hurricane was how to get gasoline. We had had no time before the storm because, as soon as the electricity went out, the gasoline pumps stopped working. On two occasions I woke up at three in the morning to get in a gas line. Wow, that was some line. We waited hours for the gasoline station to open, and then they would turn on only one pump. We filled our red gasoline jugs as much as possible to be able to pour gas into the car and move it. About twenty to thirty minutes from Manatí, in Ciales, there were pipes jutting out of the mountainside that carried water. The lines were kilometers long but it was the only place we could get water. We had to boil the water to drink, and we bathed in it. Later we were cautioned that the water could be contaminated due to animal carcasses. As for food, I had managed to buy some food and had a one-burner gas stove, but it was still difficult because you had to cook the food and eat it at that moment because there was no way to store food. If we reheated the food, it no longer had the same taste. The only things available to eat were canned sausages, canned ham, canned tuna, canned corned beef. I cannot consume any more of it to this day. No way. I eat white rice because I make it and I love it. But no one can make me eat canned corned beef, canned ham, or canned sausage. I cannot. If I have to eat it at an activity, I'll eat it and that's it. But as for me cooking it here, no. I just cannot. I also tried to get help from FEMA, but they didn't help me. I applied for five hundred dollars in aid for food about a week and a half after Maria. They said I didn't qualify. I asked for an inspection of the house, and they sent someone, but when they found out that my name was not on the deed, that the house belonged to my parents, they denied my application because they said the house was not mine[1] and I still had a mortgage. I didn't qualify for any moratoriums on house payments, nothing. It was all zero.

To be honest, I didn't want to leave the island. I had already suffered losses in my home. Neighbors were saying that people's homes were being robbed, and I was afraid, becoming very tense. We slept on inflated mattresses in the living room in order to pay attention to the passing cars and make sure no one broke into the house. Then I noticed my daughter's skin began to change color. She became very yellow, and she slept a lot, which is logical because there was nothing to do. There was no phone, no television, no nothing. There was only sleep. My son and me played a little while but she was always asleep. A military hospital arrived in Manatí and stayed a month, and I had the opportunity to take her. I wanted to alleviate my doubts be-

cause I saw her very tired. They couldn't do blood work or X-rays because
they had few supplies, only the basics. They could examine and transfer
patients. My daughter didn't have the chance to enter the hospital ship[2]
that was docked near Manatí to help patients. When we get to the military
hospital, they were very kind, very attentive, but their hands were tied. They
began talking among themselves. They put her on a cot to examine her. The
doctors and nurses were volunteers who came to help Puerto Rico. The nurse
who tended to us was from Miami and had Latino family members. She
knew how to speak Spanish, but not the doctor. He asked my daughter to
open and close her hands and stretch one of her fingers backward as much
as possible. If it became totally white, that meant her hemoglobin level was
below two digits. She had no color on her lips. He recommended that we
find a way to get her to the States as soon as possible. I had been praying
since before Irma and Maria to transfer her to the States due to her health
condition. At that moment, things changed. He said, "You have to do it. Your
daughter is dying." Dying is a big word for me because I had already lost my
mother in January. My daughter said, "There's the answer to your prayer."
My daughter is part of the American Cancer Society, and I went to their office in Hato Rey to tell them of our situation. They said they couldn't transfer
Keishla because she was not under treatment. They were transferring only
patients who were getting chemo, radiation, or dialysis.

They placed a lot of obstacles in my way, but I continued to insist. I said,
"Look at the case and the situation. She has a cerebral tumor. Her skin color
is not the same and she is becoming more debilitated. I fear for her life." The
person who tended to me had a good heart. She sent my daughter's case file
to an American Cancer Society office in Tampa, saying it would take about a
week for them to call back. I needed a hospital over here to accept Keishla's
case and agree to treat her in order for the Cancer Society to transfer her. I
left the office feeling little hope. I contacted Moffitt Cancer Center, but they
didn't accept her Puerto Rico medical plan. We waited four days. There was
no telephone communication in my area because the lines were down. I had
to drive to near the federal prison in Guaynabo to get a weak signal to let my
father's family in Ocala know that we were fine, we were alive, and also to talk
to the Cancer Society. That day I got two calls, one from someone speaking in
English and another from the person in charge of the case. It was about six

in the evening and already starting to get dark. She said, "Get ready because you leave tomorrow at seven in the morning." They would be at my house at seven to pick us up. I hadn't prepared anything. They said, "Take what you can because you're leaving. The plane will be at the Isla Grande airport at eleven in the morning. It will be a humanitarian flight."[3] The first person I heard of to take cancer patients out of Puerto Rico was Pitbull.[4]

There was no light at that hour. My flashlight had little battery life left. I could hardly see what I was doing by candlelight. We took what we could and got on the flight. We arrived on October 24, and on October 25 my daughter was in the Florida Hospital [Orlando] emergency room. There were fifteen people on the flight, patients and family members. It was a private jet with a lot of luxury. I had never traveled on a plane with such luxury in my life—the bathrooms, the seats. You could charge your phones on the arm of the seat. The seats were covered in leather, they reclined, and the tables came out of the sides. Curtains hung on the windows. It was beautiful, beautiful, beautiful. We sent blessings to the pilot and the person who provided the plane. He was Canadian and had been taking supplies to Puerto Rico and carrying patients back. He never charged for the flight. They gave us drinks and food. A medical person would check on patients. There was a reporter on the flight, and she interviewed us and captured all our faces and reactions. I was the only one who began to cry when the flight took off. I cried because I knew I was about to confront a difficult situation. I cried because I was leaving the island I love so much. I cried because I left my family behind. I visited the cemetery often to be with my parents for a while. I cried because I was afraid robbers would break into my home and take the few things I had left. I cried because I knew I wasn't going to return. I am aware that my daughter's health condition requires treatment that is different from what Puerto Rico can offer.

At the hospital, my daughter began to have respiratory problems and was unable to move. The physicians on that shift ordered a CT scan and an MRI, which showed she had a mass in her head. We knew she had a mass in Puerto Rico, but they said it was inoperable. If the mass grew, she would die because in Puerto Rico they said they couldn't operate. In Florida, all the doctors hovered over—hematologist, radiologist, oncologist. It was spectacular. She had about ten doctors treating her, all making decisions and consulting with one another. They confirmed that it's true, the mass is inoperable, but they can try radiation. She has Hodgkin's lymphoma in which a tumor never reaches the head, but in this case it did. They said her case was different. She had a clot that was nearing her heart, cancer in different parts of the body, her hemoglobin was low. They had to stabilize her and start radiation after she was discharged. She received eighteen radiation treatments on her head. In Puerto Rico she had already experienced fifty-eight radiation sessions on different parts of her body. She knew what lay ahead, with the big exception that doctors here said she would lose some of her memory and may have more intense relapses. She received her radiation, and her health improved.

When we first arrived we went to Winter Springs, in Seminole County, where we stayed for two or three weeks with a friend. From there we went to Maitland, which was close to where my daughter was being treated, to an Extended Stay hotel, from the end of October to practically March 2018, when we had to leave. A transfer specialist helped us find the lodging, which was fifteen minutes from her treatment. There were other Puerto Ricans at the Extended Stay, people who had come on earlier humanitarian flights. Some of their parents had Alzheimer's. The children were using credit cards to pay for expenses. They weren't going to let their parents starve. There were so many stories. When you did laundry, people would ask: "Where are you from? How is it going for you?" There were only a few of us but Puerto Ricans always make their presence known. When we would find each other, we would holler and yelp. Today, Keishla's tumors are smaller, but a new evaluation showed there is a tumor on the other side of her head where there had been none. So, she has two tumors, because the first one didn't completely shrink. She still has the blood clot; the cancer has moved into her bones, and she has cancer in other parts of her body again. This has not been easy.

The whole process of adjusting to Florida has been very difficult for me. First, the traffic rules in Puerto Rico are the worst, but here everything is very regulated. There are traffic cameras, while in Puerto Rico there are none. People in Puerto Rico drive how they want, where they want. Puerto Rico really doesn't have traffic laws. Not here. Everything here is about courtesy. I'm not accustomed to that. In Puerto Rico if you arrive at a stop sign, everybody tries to move at the same time. I lament to say that I already have two tickets, each for $158, that I have to deal with. I stopped on a street in

Winter Park and didn't see a camera. There was no sign telling me that I had to wait. The camera caught me twice doing the same thing. Since everybody was doing it, I figured it was right. I guess everybody got a ticket. In addition, people here are into themselves. In Puerto Rico you talk with your neighbor. You talk outside on the porches. I have had to become accustomed to the language. I understand English, but I speak very little. My children are bilingual because they attended private schools in Puerto Rico. My daughter learned English with my father and speaks without an accent. It has been more uphill for me. I can say "yes" or "thank you" or "hello," but I can't engage in a conversation. That has made things harder for me, but I just have to work on it. That has been the most difficult thing for me. I'm fascinated by the easy access to food here because that was difficult in Puerto Rico, and I know there are people still having problems getting food. My daughter has to follow a diet of fruits and vegetables, and we can find that here. That gives me peace. I'm more at peace because I know that she has all her medications and my son's education is better.

In Puerto Rico, outside of private school, the education system is terrible—maybe not the teachers but the facilities are terrible. I'm sorry to say that, because I am a product of public schools. The public schools here look like universities. When my son started school at Lockhart Middle School, he would get lost in the corridors. In Orlando he's scheduled to attend Jackson Middle School, but I'm working hard to change that. He has a lot of psychological problems because he was bullied in Puerto Rico for many years at different private schools. At Lockhart there weren't many Latinos and not too many whites. They didn't want him. They would push him and hit him on the head. Nobody spoke Spanish. The situation normalized as he spoke more English, but the fear of being bullied stayed with him. This area I live in now is not too good, and I'm trying to get him into a better school. He's already had some situations with neighbors' kids who have hit him. He makes friends with everyone and doesn't have malice. He can't discern who will do harm to him. Another thing I'm learning is not to speak too loud. I speak very loudly and fast, and when I laugh, well I'm not even going to go there. Everywhere I go people tend to look at me as if to say: "Why is she talking so loud? Why is she laughing so loud?" I don't know, maybe we Puerto Ricans are deaf and we need to speak loudly. All the people I've met, the people at my job, we all speak loudly. When we realize it we lower the volume. Maybe people can hear us outside or on the other side of the door, but in a matter of seconds we're back at it again. We roar with laughter as we relate anecdotes of the things that have happened to us.

I got this apartment through church. A fellow parishioner said there was an apartment that soon would be vacant. These apartments are condominiums. I've never had an apartment, and this has been a real blessing. My daughter is the one who negotiated with the owner, who supposedly is from Greece, and her English is not too good. But they understand each other well. I had to make a deposit and the first month's rent. It was uphill, but little by little I was able to save the money. My daughter gets Social Security through her dad because of her disability. I'm working temporarily on a project started by my priest, who proposed to help Hurricane Maria evacuees become stabilized, to get people out of the hotels. The program is called EOLA, which stands for Episcopal Office of Latino Assistance. It has been challenging and draining because the cases we get . . . if you think you're in bad shape, we meet people who are in far worse condition. But it has been gratifying to hear people say: "God bless you. Thank you for your help. Thank you for counseling me." Or, "I didn't know that." I see them go to the food pantry and take food, leaving happy and content. They can find donated clothes to wear, and we've helped many people find a place to live because we helped them land jobs. We have helped them become independent, have their own things, get an apartment and furniture. It has been very gratifying.

At some point I have to return to Puerto Rico to resolve the situation of my house because I'm very worried about that. Once that is resolved, I'm coming back. My daughter's cancer treatment doesn't have an expiration date, and my children do not want to return to Puerto Rico for anything. They say there is nothing to look forward to in Puerto Rico. Two of my daughter's friends from the island recently visited, and they had a good time, but they went back to Puerto Rico and my daughter stayed. My son says he would like to visit but not stay. I hear a lot of things on the internet and on the news that Puerto Rico is going to take twenty years to recuperate. Even then, it would return to the way it was before Maria. In twenty years I will be older, and it's going to be difficult to access health services. I don't want that. I don't want to be a burden on my children.

Glorimar Torres

Things were getting worse.

Glorimar Torres, forty-five, of Cupey, Puerto Rico, arrived in Orlando on April 28, 2018, with her twelve-year-old daughter, about six months after arranging a humanitarian flight to Florida for her sister, a nurse, and their Alzheimer's-stricken mother, eighty-one. Torres lived in an apartment in Cupey and worked at a beauty salon. In Orlando she found work at a retail store and an apartment near the Orlando attractions. Her mother lives in a nursing home.

We prepared ourselves super-well for Hurricane Irma because everyone knew the hurricane definitely was coming our way. At the last minute, it detoured away from us, and we had a smoother experience than expected. We didn't have electricity or water, but everything else appeared to operate normally. The electricity and water returned several days before Maria hit. My sister and me didn't have any recourse other than to continue to prepare better for Hurricane Maria, which they said was coming, and it would be stronger. I always prepare, even if the hurricane is not coming, contrary to many people who dismiss it saying, "Oh, the hurricane is not coming." I think Maria gave them a good lesson: You must always prepare. I had food and water, but I began to realize that you never really finish preparing, at least not for a hurricane like Maria. For all the ice, food, and stove gas that I had, everything was depleted. It didn't last even a week dividing it all between my home and my sister's.

When Maria came, some places still had no electricity. My mother was bedridden with Alzheimer's. She lived with my sister in Guaynabo in a first-floor apartment. I lived in another area, Cupey, in a second-floor apartment. I worried that her apartment would flood and suggested she come with me, but she decided to stay where she was. I spent the evening super-tense because the hurricane was moving slowly. My daughter and me were in bed together, but

Glorimar Torres

the night seemed very long as we waited for the hurricane to arrive. I heard the wind through my aluminum shutters, which seemed to heighten the noise of the wind. I woke up at six in the morning, opened my bedroom door, and saw water pouring into my living room. The wind was such that it flooded my apartment, with water coming into my living room and my three bedrooms even though my apartment had shutters. I even had tree leaves and other debris in the apartment, and, because the roof of the complex was covered with leaves, water started coming into one of my bathrooms. I was getting soaked through windows, doors, and the leaks on the roof. I began placing towels at the bottom of the doors and removed bucketloads of water. I moved furniture, anything that could be damaged. I spent nearly two days moving furniture and removing water from my apartment. When I dried out one area,

I would move furniture there and start drying another area. Thank God I had cell phone service for about a week, after which I lost it. The biggest thing I remember is when I was finally able to communicate with my sister. I learned that not a drop of water had entered my mother's room. I felt more at ease upon learning that. The hurricane ripped out the air-conditioning unit in my sister's bedroom, but nothing happened to my mother's room. If she had been with me, we would have spent the night going from room to room hauling out buckets of water. My sister lived close to the mayor's office in Guaynabo, and I think that may have helped, because her electricity would come and go, come and go. She always had water. There was a moment when I went to live with her, spending a month.

After the hurricane I was anxious to see my mother, but I couldn't leave because the fallen trees didn't allow me to leave the parking lot of my apartment. After two days I drove through Cupey, and the farthest I was able to reach was Universidad Metropolitana. I couldn't continue because there were many obstacles in my way, plus I was feeling emotional roadblocks. There is no way to prepare emotionally for this. No way. I had never seen anything like that—the light posts, the trees, the street and business signs. There was nothing green—nothing. I'm sure you may have heard about it, but to see it and live it was very sad. I saw buildings whose apartments had no windows. The sight of downed electric lines was amazing. Everything was on the ground. On the return to my apartment I saw people on the streets with saws, cutting up trees, cleaning up. I imagine that people were feeling the same desperation I was to see their family members. They had to get out. Although people on the radio were saying not to leave our homes, I think it was instinct for us to get out. Everyone must have had a reason for getting out. Mine was to see my mother. I left the apartment again on the second day, and I saw nothing: no police, no nothing. It was like being in a country that had been abandoned. I saw only people trying to get from one place to another. Following other cars, I finally reached my sister's apartment, but what normally took me fifteen minutes had taken me an hour. We formed a line of cars, sometimes going against traffic, trying not to drive over live wires. I was afraid, very nervous.

When I reached my sister's apartment, I unloaded all the emotions I was feeling. My sister hugged me and said Mami was fine, and I saw my mother.

We began seeing changes in my mother about three years ago. About a year ago she became bedridden and no longer recognized us. After the hurricane, I saw my mother every two days to economize gasoline. There were no jobs, no school. I was alone with my daughter and wanted to spend more time with my sister, my mother, my nephews, and family. The only good part of this is that I got to know my neighbors, because I had never really talked with my neighbors, and my daughter had not spent time with the other kids. Everybody was working and in the rush of going to work. I used to leave for work early in the morning. I would get my daughter and return to the apartment in the evening, tired. I think that was everybody's routine. But at that moment we realized the kids ride bicycles, they play cards, they write on the sidewalk with chalk. We became more aware that there were other things to do. We shared what we had. If someone had ice, they gave us some. If I had something cold, I would share it.

Everything was okay until I lost cell phone service. That's when desperation set in. I had friends who had sick family members and being without a means of communication made me nervous, anxious. I lost people close to me. I lost an elderly neighbor who had lung problems. I would call 911, and the ambulance would pick her up and bring her back with oxygen; then one time they couldn't come to her because it was a Sunday. How can they leave someone like her, about ninety-something years old, who needs to be in the hospital? Unfortunately, she died, and that had a big impact on me. If she had had oxygen twenty-four hours this wouldn't have happened. My best friend's mother had cancer and died just as I lost my cell phone signal. He lived in Toa Baja, where there was a lot of flooding, in a two-story house. When the rush of water came, he provided refuge to over sixteen people in the second floor of his house—children, married couples, adults, even animals. I don't know what would have happened to these people if he hadn't given them refuge. He lost everything on the first floor of his home but was able to save lives on the second floor. He had lost his father after Irma and then lost his mother after Maria. It was tragedy after tragedy. There were many losses due to those hurricanes. My nephew's father died too. He was a dialysis patient.

I realized that things were getting worse—there's no gas and my mother can only eat her food mashed; there was no Osterizer®; the Ensure® drinks are hot. She was getting dehydrated and had diarrhea. I became very concerned when she began losing weight. She had been hospitalized months earlier for a bedsore on her back. I could fit nearly my entire index finger in the bedsore. I decided we had to get her out, just as people were getting many others out. I began going on social media, listening to radio and contacting people mostly through Facebook: What did I have to do? Where did I have to go to get my mother out? I got many replies, but some others didn't respond I imagine due to the chaos. There were many sick people. My mother was not the only one. I spent two intense weeks writing messages and making calls. I needed certificates, I needed photos, I needed licenses. They wanted to know how much my mother weighed. I was living under a lot of tension because I received calls at all hours. Once I was told a humanitarian flight was leaving Aguadilla, but I had no way of getting there, of getting an ambulance to transport her. Sometimes we were notified of a humanitarian flight leaving the next day only for it to be suspended. The humanitarian flights were like that—they happened in the spur of the moment. I tried taking her to the hospital ship, but what I really wanted was to get her out of Puerto Rico so she could get medical help. Family in Florida reached out to people they knew in Puerto Rico, who then provided us with basic supplies. Some people offered to make ice for us. Others even gave us money, but nothing we had was enough, at least for my mom. Her bedsore was advanced and infected. The visiting nurse couldn't come like before. She deteriorated physically. I could see it on her face. My mother no longer smiled. She seemed sad, but perhaps she was angry or uncomfortable. Maybe she was hot; maybe she was hungry. I saw that on her face, which was thin.

The woman who helped me is Zorimar Betancourt. She is the mother of Stefano Steenbakkers, who was killed in Puerto Rico.[*] She is a warrior, and since her son was killed, she has dedicated herself to helping others with organ donations. I reached her through a friend who's a nurse and works with LifeLink, an organ donation group. The Stefano Foundation called one day at ten in the morning and said, "You're leaving, and you need to prepare to take

---

[*] Stefano Steenbakkers Betancourt, seventeen, was shot and killed during a carjacking in Puerto Rico. His organs were donated to five people, and his mother, Zorimar Betancourt, established a foundation in his name (https://www.fundacionstefano.org/foundation).

the flight." That was the moment I was waiting for, but I became paralyzed, shocked. I didn't know what to do. I started to prepare my mother's bag, but I became blocked. I didn't know what to put in her bag. I wanted to help my sister, whose son would also be on the flight. We had already sent all our information: birth certificates, driver's licenses. Everything was ready for my mother to leave. My sister saw that I was so nervous that she asked me to sit down. We had done a simulation, lifting Mami from her hospital bed and sitting her in a wheelchair to see how she was going to react. When we did that, I saw how thin she was. She had been in an accident when she was twelve years old and lost her entire left arm. I was very concerned. I had to sit down because I was trembling. I let my sister pack everything. I felt so many emotions. It's one thing to fight for two weeks to obtain something; then you have it, and it's like, "Wow." I am good at negotiating the procedures and paperwork, but this other thing I left in the hands of my sister. She is more composed, more serene. She had been studying for a master's degree in nursing and left all of that to care for our mom. I worked, and she took care of Mom.

My sister and nephews carried my mother to my car, where we strapped her into the front seat, with everybody else in the back. The flight left from Isla Grande Airport. I had little time to get to the airport because that's how this works. They call you one moment, and you have to be ready to leave. I placed my hands on the steering wheel and held on tight so I wouldn't shake. I needed to get there quickly, but I got lost at the airport due to my nerves. I didn't have information on the plane. I thought the plane would be there, but it was due to arrive. When we get to the terminal, airport employees came out to take a look at my mom. I had a lot of people calling me at that moment—from the foundation, some friends, my cousins in Florida, who wanted to know when and where my mother would arrive. Eventually they had to travel to Fort Lauderdale. The plane arrived, and we get to the tarmac. The pilot brought food for everyone on the flight, about ten people. There was a young doctor, sick and elderly people, even a service dog. I was awed by how we were treated, especially by the pilot. When he glanced at my mother, he could see she was elderly and bedridden. He took my sister on a tour of the plane and asked how we wanted my mother to travel—lying or sitting down? I have all that recorded in my memory and my cell phone. Nobody was allowed to get on the plane until my mother was situated. It was as if we were paying for the flight. Each of the people had a sense of humanity, an excellent personal touch.

Suddenly I became afraid, asking myself, "How can I put my mother on that plane?" She's elderly, has Alzheimer's, a breast cancer survivor, has only one arm, but a person who doesn't really have other ailments: no heart condition, for instance. But a maintenance worker, my sister, and me carried her up the stairs to the plane and she left. My sister left me to look after three of her five children, an eighteen-year-old and fifteen-year-old twins. She's close to her children, and I imagine she had stronger emotions than I was experiencing. She said, "Take care of them." I said, "Of course, as if they were my own." All of us were making sacrifices: my sister, my nephews, the family that received them here. Once on the plane my mother was wrapped in a sheet, and my sister said she talked the entire flight. She has been a champion all her life. I've never heard her complain. I think my sister suffered more during the flight because she was nauseous and had a headache. When they arrived in Fort Lauderdale, firefighters and rescuers were waiting because the pilot had called ahead. She flew nearly three hours on a small plane and then traveled three more hours by car to Kissimmee to a cousin's house. She's a champ. She spent several days in a hospital because she was dehydrated and had an infection. They cured her bedsore. Little by little, we began to see a change in her as she improved.

Today my mother is in a nursing home. We had to find a place for her because my sister and nephew were staying with my cousin, who lives with her in-laws. They gave her a room and set up a camper for my nephew, so we had to find a place quickly. The nursing home is not far from my cousin's home, and nursing home workers came to get her. My sister was here six months before I arrived. I felt an obligation to help her and be close to Mami. It took me a while to get here because I was preparing myself emotionally and financially to come to Florida. I was trying to support everyone emotionally and financially from Puerto Rico. I had to sell everything I had, not knowing what I would face here. She would call and ask, "When are you coming?" Each time we did FaceTime I cried. My sister said, "I'm not calling you anymore because you always cry." I really missed my family. In Puerto Rico there may have been five or six days when I didn't see them, but we always called each other. I knew if I got in the car I could get to my sister's house in minutes and they'd be there. But I was alone with my daughter and my three nephews. I perceived my sister's anxiety because she was without her children. There were no airline flights. It was chaos at the airport with flight cancellations. She struggled with that until she finally bought tickets for the fifteen-year-old twins. A lot of people were leaving, and I remember going to the airport often to take so many friends and family. My other nephew went to South Dakota to work. I have a twenty-seven-year-old son who left to work in Tennessee in November 2017. That was another drive to the airport, another set of good-byes. It felt as if I were experiencing many losses every time somebody left the island, every time someone close to me died.

Maria changed my life. I had been working a couple of months with my Toa Baja friend who lost his parents. He was my boss, my friend, my brother. It was tough to leave him. I experienced a lot of things up close and began to think of all the losses. I wanted to leave Puerto Rico while at the same time I didn't want to leave, but I knew I had to do it. All my family is in Florida. I sold off my things one by one. The bed and television were the last to go. I arrived in Orlando on April 28, 2018. My sister had rented a studio apartment, and at one moment there were about seven of us in the little studio. That's when all the changes in my life started. We took turns on the floor, on the sofa, on the air mattress. The lease expired at the end of June, and I was waiting on this apartment, so we began searching for a hotel. The Episcopal Church found us an Airbnb apartment with two bedrooms for two days. It was very beautiful. We had all our things in our cars. Then a friend told us about a hotel on Orange Blossom Trail. It was terrible, but I paid for the hotel, and we stayed three weeks. They were the longest three weeks of our lives. It was dirty, cockroaches, people smoking, garbage. One day my sister called to say a man was hitting a woman. But it was two beds. We had hot food from the church people, who would come, pray, and sing with us. They brought roast chicken, rice, and beans. They brought a cooler with ice and water. They even brought us toothbrushes and, one time, donuts. The church couldn't have done more for us. We left that hotel for another, better hotel. It was three days here, and three days there. My daughter's grandmother asked us to go with her, and the hotel returned some of my money. Then I got the call that my apartment was ready, so we were with her only two days.

My sister found a job as a nurse in South Dakota, but she didn't want to tell me. That was a terrible week for me. I spent it crying. It was a real big hit. I felt that she was leaving me after asking me to come here. We each moved into our apartments on the same day in different states. We did a FaceTime, and I started to cry, but I was able to see that she was happy. At the new apartment we slept two weeks on the carpeted floor. The church referred me to Mustard Seed,* and for $150 I was able to get two beds. I got a lot of other things out of there: a crib, a patio set, and a fryer—all of which I gave away. I knew a lot of people who came and maybe couldn't afford the $150. A person I met at CareerSource gave me a TV and a microwave.

I feel fine now, and I'm working two jobs, twenty hours at Marshalls and twelve hours at Macy's, more than thirty hours with both jobs. Marshalls may offer me a full-time position. That job has been a blessing, and I'm very excited. It's a new store, and it's like seeing it being born. It's a great feeling. Macy's had cut my hours, and when my coworkers didn't see me at Macy's, they called to ask how I was. They made me feel super because I am alone here with my daughter. But working two jobs is hard. I lose sleep. Sometimes I can't see my mom, so when I'm free I go straight to the nursing home. As the hurricane anniversary neared, I became a little sensitive, like a flashback, and became anxious when I heard about Hurricane Florence. I went to the doctor's because I was very depressed and had a headache, high blood pressure, and I was dehydrated. I paid twelve dollars for the medication because I have no medical plan.

I would like to visit Puerto Rico and see a few close friends, but I would return to Orlando. My daughter's schooling is better here. Her old school had no electricity, and she spent four months out of school. She has attention deficit [disorder], and she is improving. She understands what they ask her in English. She has tutoring. The bus comes to get her. There are so many things for her to do here. My life for the time being is here in Orlando. I don't think I will move from here, not to South Dakota, where my sister is, or Tennessee, where my son is. My mother is here. She has gained weight and looks super-good. I have a roof over my head and pay my rent. I have two jobs. The only thing I'm missing is speaking better English.

---

* Mustard Seed of Central Florida is a furniture and clothing bank for the economically disadvantaged.

Ivelisse Marrero

We woke up to a destroyed Puerto Rico.

Ivelisse Marrero, forty-seven, was born in Ponce and raised north of Ponce in Villalba, as well as in Boston, Massachusetts, where she lived from ages fifteen to thirty-two. In 2003 she returned to Puerto Rico, residing in Caguas, which is just south of metropolitan San Juan, until October 2017 after Hurricane Maria. A former insurance agent, she has three children ages twenty-nine, twenty-six, and eighteen, the youngest of whom she sent to Tampa before the hurricane in July 2017 to finish high school. Marrero has three sisters in Florida and has visited Florida many times. She thought of Florida, particularly the Orlando-Kissimmee area, as a place to retire but, until now, not to live.

I spent Hurricane Irma with a friend in Carolina. That was the first hurricane I had experienced because my parents would often bring us to the States when I was a child, and I never lived through a hurricane in Puerto Rico. Irma didn't cause much damage in the Carolina area, at least not where I was, although it did leave some wreckage in the Loíza and Fajardo areas. Maria was totally traumatizing and also depressing. I had returned to Caguas, and that's when they announced that another hurricane was coming. Obviously, we thought nothing would happen, as had occurred with Irma. For many people the hurricane experience is like crying wolf, but the wolf never arrives. We have been blessed for many years, praying that hurricanes would not touch us, and they bypassed us. But Maria was different. I first realized that something strong was coming when I saw the face of meteorologist Ada Monzón.* Her body language told me that this is serious. Then I heard First Lady Beatriz Rosselló announce that we

---

* Ada Monzón is a well-known meteorologist in Puerto Rico who works with WIPR-TV, WKAQ radio, and Noticel. In 2018, she won an award for broadcast meteorology from the American Meteorological Association for her "long-term commitment to educating, informing, and inspiring resiliency in the people of Puerto Rico before, during, and after extreme events like Hurricane María."

should prepare ourselves. I closed my apartment in Caguas; we put tape over all the glass windows, thinking that water would come in or they wouldn't be able to withstand the wind, and I spent Hurricane Maria at my son's house in Gurabo. We were all there—my son, his girlfriend, my daughter, her two children, and me. My daughter and her two children lived with me. We closed the front door and the door to the hall and went to a bedroom. At one in the morning the wind woke me up, and water started coming in through the windows. It sounded like a wolf or lion. It is growling so strongly. We were afraid since we didn't know if we would live or die. We closed the doors to the bedrooms and all moved to a small hallway where there were no windows. That's where we spent the hurricane. We had been texting our family here in Florida but lost communication between two and three in the morning. We didn't hear from them or they from us until nearly a week later.

We went to sleep that night in beautiful and gorgeous Puerto Rico and woke up to a destroyed Puerto Rico. We didn't leave the apartment the day after the hurricane because the roads were impassable. Trees and light posts were strewn all over the roads. But the following day, as people began cleaning up, I went back to Caguas, and it was traumatizing. It was as if an atomic bomb had gone off in Puerto Rico. Everything looked burned. Cement posts had fallen on the main streets of Caguas. The gasoline stations had been destroyed. It was very depressing. I never imagined I would live through something like that. Never. We started walking through the streets of Caguas to see what had happened. I was in shock. To get to my apartment we had to get out of the car to remove trees in our path. When we finally entered my apartment, I don't know if it's the faith that I have—I had prayed before leaving, "God, You are going to take care of this"—but my apartment was dry, not one drop of water, and I had broken windows. I had texted my next-door neighbor with whom I share a wall, and she had been emptying buckets of water throughout the night. I said, "My God, thank you." Such is faith.

Since we hadn't really prepared ourselves, my daughter, kids, and me went out to look for food. We didn't have water or electricity either. Thank God we found an open supermarket and got in line for an hour and managed to get inside. Soon afterward, they closed the supermarket. I felt such a huge hurt inside of me because they wouldn't allow people to come in, and they were begging. But there was no electricity, and employees couldn't stay late. They had

Ivelisse Marrero

to return to their homes. We were able to buy some groceries. My son-in-law brought us a one-burner gas stove, and we were able to cook. We had nothing cold because I refused to get in one of those long lines to get ice, which was only going to melt in two to three hours. Everything we drank was hot. I was able to drink something cold maybe fifteen days after the hurricane. The lines to buy gas lasted hours and hours. A man committed suicide at a gas station out of desperation. I didn't see it, but I heard it on the news. The desperation was very grave. In Puerto Rico, the number of people with mental illnesses and depression is big. Puerto Rico has had its head down many years: the economy, all the things people have suffered. I don't want to talk bad about any political party, but the truth is, we have to take the reins of Puerto Rico. No matter the political party all have done the same things for many years. The deaths that were justified are not certain. There was much more than that. Thousands and thousands and thousands of deaths. A lot of things you all saw here we couldn't see over there because, obviously, we had no TV, no methods of communication. But people here saw everything. There were things I learned after I got here, like the ladies who died buried in their house.[5] There were lots of things we didn't know because of the lack of communication.

I had a nonprofit in Puerto Rico called Blue Butterflies to help single parents. It was the first such foundation in Puerto Rico that included single fathers, because all the foundations and organizations are pro-women. But what about the men? They also play a role in our lives. I was a single mother for many years, and I wanted to help them reach their goals and dreams. I also was depressed for ten years, and I wanted to help women and men to come out of depression. I had the idea to help broken families get along better, because sometimes the mother talks bad about the father or the father talks bad about the mom. That shouldn't happen because children are the ones who suffer. I come from a broken family and lived with an alcoholic stepfather. There was a lot of emotional abuse and domestic violence. I wanted to help families avoid that and learn how to talk with their children. I met my children's father when I was fourteen, and we were married when I was sixteen. I kept going from there. I studied life coaching; I studied counseling. When Maria hit, I was working as an insurance agent on commission, but after the hurricane, who was going to buy health insurance at that moment? Nobody. Since people weren't prepared for the hurricane, their money went toward buying portable generators, gasoline, and food. No one was thinking of buying insurance. What to do? I thought of my grandchildren. I didn't want them to lack any necessities. A friend called to say FEMA was recruiting interpreters paying forty dollars an hour. I said, "Lord, if it's for me to stay here, they'll give me the job." I already had a plane ticket for the next day for Orlando. When I get to the San Juan Convention Center—that's where everybody was—they wouldn't let me inside. I insisted that I had an appointment, and after a half hour I was allowed in. I interviewed, and the woman says I have to pass a background check. She asked that I leave my information even though I said I had a flight the next day. I left on October 10 for Orlando. I have three sisters here, and one of them paid for our tickets. We all came. My son and his girlfriend stayed with my nephew. Me and my grandchildren went to my sister's house in Kissimmee. I passed through the evacuee Resource Center at the airport and applied for food stamps. I looked for jobs on indeed.com, but nobody was calling me. Then I learned they were sending me appointments through email. I never looked at my email. I was half-depressed myself with all the trauma. One day I get up and say, "Today I'm going to find a job." I went to CareerSource, and they pointed me to the computers. After two and a half hours I'm thinking I could have done this at home. I thought someone was going to sit down with me and help me find a position. As I'm leaving, I saw a well-dressed Puerto Rican woman—I knew she was Puerto Rican because Puerto Ricans can just tell—and asked if she was helping people find jobs. She said she was helping evacuees from Irma and Maria. An earlier group had gone into a room for orientation, and she asked me to wait for the next session. They would pay me fifteen dollars an hour. I didn't ask for what. I said, "I'll wait three hours if I have to."

I was placed to work at Good Samaritan near Intercession City. I didn't know who they were, and I didn't have a car. When I told my sister the news, she said, "Oh, that's right here in front." I said, "This is the hand of God." I didn't have a car, and it was right in front of my sister's place. I could walk it. I started to work from seven in the morning to three thirty in the afternoon, but my sister didn't want me to walk in the dark. The first couple of days a coworker gave me a lift. Then my sister loaned me one of her cars. I finished the internship in two and half months. We did everything: housekeeping, landscaping, moving. Name it, we did it. I took off my heels; I put on a pair of jeans and sneakers and a T-shirt; sometimes I wore a hat and didn't even comb my hair or wear makeup. I said, "Let's do what we have to do." I was placed in the department of environmental services. There were eight other Maria evacuees. We cleaned centers, we cleaned bathrooms, we cleaned apartments. We moved people's furniture. We put it in storage and we took it out of storage. When it was slow, I begged them to give me an assignment because I am real hyper. I have to be doing something. They put me in landscaping where we were pulling palm tree leaves, and that's hard.

We would be pulling palm leaves and sometimes the guys—sorry, guys—would just sit and watch us. It was hard work, but we did what we had to do. If you have to start from the bottom, then start at the bottom. At some point you'll have to rise again. After that, we fell into a limbo. I spent a month locked inside my home depressed. Then I get a call from a Venezuelan friend I worked with at Good Samaritan who said CareerSource was looking to interview me. I was literally in bed, depressed. I got up and got dressed as if I were going to work and left. They placed me at the Kissimmee Chamber of Commerce, where I stayed two months. I learned a lot there. They treated me very well and wrote me a great letter of recommendation. I began to feel emotionally better when I began working at the Kissimmee Chamber of Commerce. I know that when God has a purpose, He will place you in the perfect place to learn what you have to learn so you can fulfill your purpose.

Later CareerSource called me about a position to help other Puerto Ricans find work. I didn't know whether to laugh or cry. I was so emotional. I left Puerto Rico, but I didn't really want to leave. I felt that I needed to help my people in Puerto Rico, but I couldn't generate income. In that job I helped connect people with resources: United Way, Mustard Seed. Thanks to my experiences in Puerto Rico and everything I learned, I could do this job. Lamentably, however, I was there only eighty-nine days. I have interviewed with many people and have some offers because I met many people. I relate to everybody and talk with everyone. I still help people who I was trying to help at Career-Source. My big dream is to be a motivational speaker. I am writing a book about my experiences after Hurricane Maria and, at some point, would love to form an organization like Goodwill to help others. That's my big dream.

It was difficult for me to get used to Florida in the beginning, but now I think it's paradise. My difficulty was that I hadn't planned to come here. I left Puerto Rico suddenly, leaving everything behind. I felt that my goals and dreams would die in Puerto Rico. But I also felt a strong pull to come to Florida even though I didn't want to be here. I always say that wherever God directs my life that's where I have to be. Today I know a lot of people. I'm finding a lot of people here who I knew in Puerto Rico. I don't feel as if I left Puerto Rico because on every corner I'm bumping into someone I know. I found a friend who had worked at OfficeMax in Caguas at the OfficeMax here.

What I love about Florida is the higher quality of life. Yes, it's more expensive here, but there's quality of life. In Puerto Rico we paid tolls, and the highways were all broken. If you went to a government office it took all day for someone to tend to you, and maybe they couldn't resolve your issue. Here, people help you right away, even with an email or call. There is more peace here. Today my son has an apartment with his girlfriend, and they each have jobs and cars. He speaks English because he's bilingual; she hardly speaks English but isn't afraid to learn. They are doing well. My daughter returned to Puerto Rico with her two children. She's a single mom, has an apartment, a car, and a job. Here it's not like Puerto Rico. You cannot live off the government. That is Puerto Rico's big flaw, that so many people live off government, *el mantengo*. Sometimes I would go to the motels to help people find jobs through Career-Source, and some would tell me, "Don't find me a job where I work too hard because my back hurts." You can't survive like that here. I was called to clean a house on Saturday, and that's what I'm going to do. If I have to wash cars, that's what I'll do because I wash my own car. You have to do what you have to do to survive. I will do what I have to for a better quality of life.

Margarita Rodríguez Guzmán

Puerto Rico returned to the 1940s.

Margarita Rodríguez Guzmán, fifty-two, is from Caguas, Puerto Rico, and was living in Orlando for six months with her mother and stepfather, who owned a home in south Orlando. Margarita arrived in Florida on November 8, 2017, with her husband and two chihuahua therapy dogs in tow. She was excited because she would soon begin work at a Hyatt hotel after making plans and setting goals for what she wanted to accomplish. She recalled in excruciating detail the turbulence and desperation she experienced trying to reestablish a sense of normalcy after Hurricane Maria.

We lived in a rented apartment in Caguas, Puerto Rico. Hurricane Irma was not as severe as Hurricane Maria, but I still lost electricity and water, and when Maria hit a week later, the utilities still hadn't been turned on. I was without light and water until November 8, 2017, the day I left Puerto Rico for Florida. People tell me that even today there is no water or electricity in the same neighborhood. People are surviving with generators. The apartment was not destroyed because it was constructed of cement, but the windows were old and the water came in with a lot of force. There were open spaces between the wall and the sides of the windows, and water came in and left a trail on the floor. My screen door was blown off, and the water entered through there. I tried placing our clothes on the windows so they could absorb the water, but I ended up throwing out those clothes because they smelled. I filled a drum outside the apartment with the clothes. The air-conditioning developed mold. Everything got wet. My husband's sleep apnea machine was damaged. I sent all my photos to FEMA, but after I arrived here they denied my application. I told my husband, anything they give us will help. I don't need luxury to survive. I appealed my case to FEMA to recover damages for what I lost, but they denied me a second time. If it weren't for my mother, father, and stepfather, I wouldn't have survived.

We thought Hurricane Maria was going to be like Irma, but it didn't turn out that way. Maria didn't give us time to prepare. Hurricane Maria came from another world. The noise was deafening; it made you crazy because that's all you could hear. The winds started up at eight that night, and you could still hear the winds at noon the next day. There was no calm even when the eye of the storm passed over Caguas. You heard, "wooo, wooo, wooo." It was deafening. The storm yanked out trees and a cistern. I peeked out the bathroom window and could see the trees blowing away. If a tree like that hit you, it would kill you. The quenepa trees outside my apartment all fell on top of one another. I told my husband, "Let's take advantage and make a clothing line." I would wake up at two or three in the morning to wash clothes, and that's where I hung them. I had no water for the toilets. I filled the car trunk with empty plastic jugs and went looking for water wherever there were water pipes on the roadside. I woke up every day and looked for water. I was able to use my car, but I spent a lot of time in my garage patching up my tires because there were a lot of nails and screws on the roads. I went to a tire repair place, and there were over fifteen vehicles ahead of me. Everybody was going through the same thing. People were very desperate. You could see it on their faces,

Margarita Rodríguez Guzmán

especially the elderly. People were suffering. I told my husband, "It's dangerous to drive out there." There were fallen trees and electric poles, and you didn't know which had a live wire.

When I opened the door of my apartment after the hurricane, I saw a different world. You could see the most minimal movement on the mountains, which looked burned. I drove to Route 172 in Caguas to see how the mountains looked. It was desolate. I went to Barrio Cañaboncito to a friend's house and, *bendito*, I was saddened by what I saw. Her grandmother's wooden house was no longer there. The refrigerator had landed in the middle of the road. They had to take her out of there. She recently sent me a photo saying they are rebuilding the house, but they still had no water or electricity. I went to Río Piedras before and after the hurricane to buy a generator, but when I got there at three in the morning there was a tremendous line, and I was one-hundred-something on the list. That was before the hurricane. We returned after Maria, and the line had more than doubled to over three hundred people. I couldn't buy a generator—one generator was priced at ten thousand dollars. My situation was such that I couldn't finance it. I said to myself, "I'll use candles and flashlights," and that's what I did. Until I left Puerto Rico on November 8, I was buying candles and batteries. To pass the early evening hours my husband adapted a charger to connect the car battery to the DVD, and that's how we watched movies. A friend sold me all his DVDs, and that's what we did each night, sometimes falling asleep in the car. But the mosquitoes wouldn't leave us alone. When you turned on the car lights, you'd see the hungry mosquitoes buzzing everywhere. If not for those movies, we would have died of desperation. The apartment was too hot. You felt the heat the most after the hurricane passed. It was unbearable. I slept with a handheld fan all the time.

One time Duracell came to Caguas City Hall, and I went to get batteries. I also ate there because they were giving out lunch. A group called Urbe a pie started a volunteer food bank, and anyone who wanted to help feed the town could do so. People brought food from home, and it was divided up for everyone. I had groceries and took some over there before it all went bad. My freezer was full of *sofrito, pasteles,* and candy. I gave it away.

When it rained at three in the morning, my husband would go downstairs to shower under the gutter spout in the dark. He would say, "Come join me," but I said no. It was so dark you couldn't see anything. I was scared of the dark. It was black, black, black. You couldn't distinguish if someone was coming. And if you went outside you had to light a repellant coil because the mosquitoes were hungry on top of you. We filled containers of water from that spout each time it rained to flush the toilets and to bathe. It was clean water. That's how we solved problems. The apartment owner gave me water from her well. She said, "Come quietly because the neighbors are already complaining." You see, it was a neighborhood well. She gave me water about two or three times. But then the water service returned in my mother-in-law's house, and I was there all the time. Water is something essential. It's more important than electricity. Before we left Puerto Rico, I gave my mother-in-law all my plastic jugs because the water service would still come and go. There were days when you had it and days when you didn't. But electricity—nothing, ever.

The Pittsburgh Pirates came to our town[6] to help us about two to three weeks after the hurricane. Over 1,500 people showed up at the local stadium. There were a lot of elderly people there. It was very depressing. People were so disillusioned. What I saw I don't wish on anybody. The Pirates have a farm team in our area, the Criollos de Caguas. They sent a lot of supplies to the team. I received an enormous amount of groceries—rice, spaghetti, soup, soap, Chubbs®, batteries, flashlights, a big bottle of hand sanitizer. Everything was in cans. I got canned rice. I'd never seen anything like that. They even gave me fifty pounds of dog food. They brought dog food because many people didn't have money to buy it. They brought water too. When I saw those bottles of water. . . . They gave me ten bottles of water, oh! I took two bottles to my elderly neighbor, and I made him a plate of *jamonilla* [canned ham]. "That is gold," he said when he saw the bottles of water. Nobody was taking anything to him. But Puerto Ricans always share. We share like brothers and sisters. That is one of our characteristics because we are very united. I noticed while waiting in lines that people talked with one another, saying, "I have this. If I can help you, I'm here." I like to talk with people a lot. I would spend eight to nine hours in line to get gas, but I took a chair and an umbrella to sit under and listen to everybody. Sometimes you didn't want to leave because we were socializing.

Once I visited an uncle in Ponce to check on how he was doing, and I stopped at a Burger King. I tell you, I waited an hour and a half in Burger King just to place an order. We ate the food in five minutes. We had to hurry because other people wanted to sit. It was so full. Imagine, they closed the Burger King, and the line was still all the way outside. An employee stood by the door allowing only a certain number of people in at a time.

I went to Barrio Morales, where they were giving out water filters because

some water was contaminated, and I saw doctors tending to patients at an outdoor basketball court because at that moment the hospitals weren't tending to
anyone. I took my husband because his sugar level was as high as the clouds.
There were about twenty people there. Some people had headaches; others had
stress. Everything was closed at the time. My own doctor was tending patients
in his waiting room without electricity. Sometimes he would tend to patients
in their cars with the air-conditioning on. He said, "Come one by one," and he
would hand out prescriptions like in the old days. Puerto Rico returned to the
1940s with this hurricane. A guy who worked at a funeral home in Caguas told
me that a lot of people died because of the hurricane. The corpses were turning
green, and the funeral home couldn't accept any more. They had to bury them
right away. You died and they buried you without a service because there was
no time. Many people died. Many, many people. I heard a comment while I was
waiting in a line that a person died during the hurricane and spent many days
in the house in a bed. He started to give off liquids, and the family had to bury
him in their backyard. At least it was out in the country. There are still areas out
in the country that people haven't reached. I tell you this because I went to the
rural area where I used to live, and there were a lot of desperate people, elderly
people, and a lot of frustration. What happened in Puerto Rico was something
extraordinary. I experienced Hurricane Hugo, and it was in no way like Hurricane Maria. Nothing, nothing, nothing was the same.

I worked parking cars for two years, but I lost the job when the owner
didn't reopen the business after the hurricane. We depended on the restaurant next door for clients, and when the restaurant closed, we had to close
too. They had an enormous generator, but it was damaged, and there was
no way to get parts. I handed over the keys to my car to the bank, not because I wanted to, but for my peace of mind. They gave me a moratorium on
payments. I explained I didn't have a job, and she said, "Come back and get
another moratorium." When I realized I wasn't going to get a job, I couldn't
hold onto the car, and that's when I realized we had to leave Puerto Rico. I
spoke with my mother and stepfather, and they said, "Yes, come." We immediately bought tickets and came through Fort Lauderdale because I couldn't
find tickets to Orlando. We arrived early in the morning, and as soon as I got
here I went to Orlando International to look for help. My husband changed
his driver's license, I got a Florida ID, we got food stamps, my husband did a

Social Security change of address, and I opened an account with Chase. We did everything in a couple of hours. After that I came back to sleep. I hadn't been able to sleep in Puerto Rico since the hurricane.

I did everything else little by little. I attended a welcome workshop in Orlando, Talleres de Bienvenida.[*] It was very educational. They explained a lot of things step-by-step, and now I understand a lot of things: rents are high and you have to have excellent credit. My husband lost a house in Puerto Rico, and there are some old things on my credit record as well. A Hispanic Federation[†] lawyer is helping me improve my credit. I start working and studying next week. I had a lot of interviews and papers to fill out, and CareerSource[‡] helped me a lot. I did my résumé there and sent it out to jobs using their computers. They offer a lot of help. I look on the internet a lot. I found the Talleres on the internet and signed up with my husband. I have done things little by little. My husband has doctors now. He has severe apnea, neuropathy, diabetes—he has a lot of conditions. He got very ill during and after the hurricane. I don't have medical insurance, but I hope to soon. I'm going to study culinary arts because I love to cook. I worked eleven years in different restaurants in Puerto Rico, the last five of those years catering. I interviewed at the Hyatt by International Drive and will be reporting there next week at eight in the morning. They will train and pay me. I earn a certificate after three months. I hope to stay there, or at least get a recommendation to another job.

I'm not looking back; I'm looking forward. I'm not one of these people who sits around waiting. I have to do everything. I've always been that way. I have all my family here—my sister and nieces and nephews—but I can't depend on them because they work, and each one makes their own life. They've lived here a long while. I have to learn because the way Puerto Rico is going, I cannot return there. Puerto Rico is not in my thoughts now. I was

---

[*] Talleres de Bienvenida is a program started in 2014 by Samí Haiman Marrero of Orlando to provide Hispanic newcomers with orientation and information on living and working in the Orlando area. It has conducted dozens of workshops for more than eight hundred newcomers. Nancy Rosado, *Tossed to the Wind* collaborator, is a member of the board of directors.

[†] The Hispanic Federation is the Orlando offshoot of a New York–based nonprofit group. It launched various programs to help Hurricane Maria survivors.

[‡] CareerSource Central Florida is a workforce development, job training, and placement service that is part of the Florida Department of Economic Opportunity.

born there, and I love Puerto Rico, but for now I don't think of returning. The island of Puerto Rico is going to empty out because young people are leaving, and the ones who are staying behind are the elderly because they can't or won't leave.

Many things are different here. I find that everything is far. In Puerto Rico everything is near you. I worked five minutes from my job. Here, without a car you can't move around. When I interviewed at the Hyatt the first thing they asked me was, "Do you have a car?" My mother helped cosign for a car so I can go to work. A car here is not a luxury but a necessity. I once walked from here to a nearby mall, and my tongue almost fell out. You can't walk from here to there, especially if it's hot.

But everything is possible if you have faith and you want to achieve it. You have to persevere. But if you stay in your home and don't do anything, no. I'm not that kind of person. My next goal is to find an apartment. Work, save money, and get an apartment. I think it will take six months once I start working. It doesn't matter where. I'm a peaceful person. I love it here because it's peaceful. I also like Tavares, in Lake County, where my niece lives, because it's country. There have been moments when I've been desperate, depressed, but I have a lot of faith. I have my car and my job. God is good.

Coralis Alméstica Cintrón

The experience was a good one for young people.

Coralis Alméstica Cintrón, twenty, is a University of Puerto Rico student from Sierra Bayamón, Puerto Rico, who lived with her grandmother at the time of Hurricane Maria. She left Puerto Rico after the hurricane, leaving her elderly grandmother behind. She arrived first in Georgia, where her mother lived, and later settled in Orlando, where she is a second-year student at Valencia College, studying business administration. She also works a part-time job at a hotel. She hopes to transfer to the University of Central Florida to finish her bachelor's degree.

Coralis Alméstica Cintrón

I was born in Orlando, curiously enough, but my parents separated when I was one month old, and I went to live in Puerto Rico. That's why my culture and language are from the island. I was raised by my grandmother and my great-grandmother in a house in Bayamón. We prepared more for Hurricane Irma, but it was not what we expected. Irma didn't do much to us. We were without electricity, but it arrived before Maria hit. Unfortunately, it lasted only a week. So for the second hurricane we stocked up on supplies we had used up for Irma. For Maria my mentality was that nothing was going to happen; maybe the damages would be fewer than for Irma. But for Maria I was missing lots of things in the house—drinking water, for instance. I think my grandmother, who is seventy-five years old, thought she had bought a certain quantity, and there was not good communication, so we didn't have water during the hurricane. She was very nervous, and I had to use a lot of psychology with her. The aluminum roof of the terrace blew away, and that's why she was so nervous. The terrace is close to the room we were in. That was the view we saw from the room, and it left a big impression on her. Some doors were destroyed by the wind, but thank God we were all in good health. The impact was emotional. My grandmother lost a lot of weight, about fifteen pounds. I did too. I lost about twenty-five pounds. I've regained maybe five pounds since then.

Nobody came to help us, but thanks to our extraordinary neighbors who were always there for us, we were able to replace our supplies. I didn't expect much from the government. The year 2017 was a year of many problems in Puerto Rico, and I felt they had other priorities than to be asking me if I was OK or not. That's my way of thinking. It was a good lesson in survival. I would go walking through the neighborhood asking, "Who has this and that?" We were lacking ice right away, and gasoline was in short supply. If you ran out of food in your home, you had to eat out and needed to use the car, but there was no gasoline. I remember one day getting in line with friends to buy gasoline in Palo Seco near Highway 165 at four in the morning and waiting until five in the afternoon. We were never able to buy gas. We were there twelve hours and never got any gas! It was horrible. The next day we went to another gas station, in Cataño, and waited six hours. Luckily, we were able to buy gas.

This experience was a good one for young people. We had to set aside our pride, forget about what people will say or think. A lot of people don't reach out to others. They say, let him or her look for me first. After Maria, that pride disappeared among my friends. We would call to check on each other, asking, "How are you?" There was none of that pride about who reaches out to whom first. It was natural to be concerned for everyone. Everyone had the initiative to reach out without fear or timidity. We were not ashamed. On the contrary, it was such a difficult experience that we helped each other more. I had friends in Toa Baja—Levittown—where the lake level rose. We used kayaks to rescue some friends. It's something you never imagined you would have to do: rescue a friend from a house under ten feet of water. That's something you imagine only in the movies. We learned that it was important to be united. Oftentimes you think you have to do everything yourself, and we learned to use each other as resources. That's what we did. This person looked for gas, that person looked for water. We all worked as a team, which in reality is how we ought to work every day. It was an experience that taught us we need to work together and ask, "How is the best way to work?"

I know that my grandmother was affected when I left because we have always lived together. She saw it as, "Wow, you're not here because of Hurricane Maria." In reality, that's not the case. I see it as something bad that happened, but other doors opened for me. In Puerto Rico, the situation was grave since way before Maria with the fiscal control board. As a student at the University of Puerto Rico, this affected me a great deal. Students don't go to class, and the professors practically don't either. They go on strike, and that affects me academically. I don't criticize their purpose, but I have goals to fulfill. My life is not focused on protesting but on establishing myself in my profession. That's why I came here. The path is more viable here. I find the path shorter in the States compared with Puerto Rico, where too many doors were closed to me. I had a big argument with one of my best friends during the hurricane because we were no longer understanding each other. It was a very strong discussion. Our interests had changed, and that's what pushed me to leave Puerto Rico. We have known each other all our lives. We were neighbors and grew up together from the time we were in Pampers®. He made a comment as if to say my grandmother was a freeloader. He had said that to me once before. This is a person who doesn't have many friends. This situation made me aware of a lot of things, to see the world from another perspective. It was the factor that made me say, "I'm leaving." It was a difficult decision to make. I ended the friendship, and that gave me the chance to meet other great people. Everything is going super. I have no regrets. I left Puerto Rico on October 1, 2017, and went to Lawrenceville, Georgia, where my mother lives. She works for a medical insurance company and also is a translator. I was there two months, until the end of November. I moved to Orlando to study at Valencia College. I didn't like Lawrenceville. There were a lot of Latinos, but there are many more here. I didn't like the culture there. Everything was study and work. There was no entertainment. There was no place where you could go to relax, at least not that I could find. I can't live there. It's a great state to make money. There are a lot of jobs there, a lot of opportunities. Anyone who says there are no opportunities in Lawrenceville is lying. I found a job working at Metro PCS, and I found it quickly. Other companies were calling offering me jobs as well. It's an excellent place to earn money. But Orlando was offering more help to evacuees. I have family and friends here. My mother and me drove twelve hours from Georgia in a Dodge van she borrowed from her boyfriend. Once here, we stayed with a close friend of my mother's for a week. I had to return to Puerto Rico to get college transcripts and other documents, and I needed clothes. I didn't leave Puerto Rico empty-handed, but I didn't bring the things I needed to live. I didn't leave Puerto Rico with the idea of staying out here four or five years. I left with the illusion of returning to Puerto Rico. I love Puerto Rico. Apart from all the destruction on the island, Puerto Rico for me continues to be a beautiful place. In a year or two, it will be totally green again. I wouldn't change it for anything, but for me it's a step backward. I don't know if other people feel this way, but I do. I tell all my friends that Orlando is my bootcamp, allowing me to establish myself in my profession and give myself the things or luxuries I want. I don't want to be just middle class like my family. I want more. I stayed one month in Puerto Rico, and when I returned to Orlando in January 2018 I stayed with my mother's friend again. Within two days I had signed the lease for this apartment.

In the week my mother and me stayed with her friend we had planned out everything. We planned for the apartment, and I registered at Valencia College. Everything had been done. It was only a matter of my signing the paperwork. I'm taking twelve credits per semester, and I'm working. I took an English proficiency test and came out average. I know English—I understand it and can write it—but I'm not super-fluent. I began looking for a job and my roommate too. She also left Puerto Rico after Hurricane Maria, and I found her after I placed an announcement on Twitter in Puerto Rico. I wrote, "I need a roommate to live with me because I want to get out of my house." It was not too serious, but she replied, saying: "I want to leave too because I'm tired of my parents. I want to be an adult. I want to be independent and I don't want to live under their roof anymore." It turns out that I knew her because we had taken gymnastics class together, but we weren't close. While we were both looking for work in Orlando, she got a call from two jobs. She accepted a job as a gymnastics trainer and referred me to a hotel job. She couldn't work two jobs since she's taking nineteen credits. She's one of the best cheerleaders from Puerto Rico, and she wants to be on the cheer team for UCF. She cannot take on so much work; it would distract from her goal. Frankly, she has more opportunities here than me because of her sport. I have been able to learn from her. She was super-excited when she told me about the hotel job, saying, "Get dressed. I'm going to take you to the hotel." I was interviewed and got the job. That was in February.

Orlando has opened its doors to me. It has given me a real hand. I have a Pell Grant, and I received some funds due to Hurricane Maria. It went directly into my bank account. It said, "Hurricane Maria help." All of the assistance I have received has been through Valencia College. We have a Valencia counselor who is amazing; she is excellent. She has taken it upon herself to practically organize our lives. She has searched for economic help for us. I joke that she's working on commission, but she says no. She's an excellent worker. I hope to transfer to UCF in 2019. There is a group of students, about ten or twelve, from Puerto Rico who all came after Maria, and we hang out together. We eat out a lot, sometimes we play games, sometimes we drink, sometimes we go exercise at the UCF gym. We have to do crazy things in order to buy liquor because we are underage.[*] We are all in our first to third year of university. We get together all the time. I have met up with people who I studied with in Puerto Rico, and I say to myself, "Wow, what a coincidence that I would meet up with them here." That's how we have connected and how we have come to realize how small Puerto Rico is, because I have met up with at least ten people who I know from Puerto Rico.

In the long term I don't think I'll stay in Orlando. I would like to experi-

---

[*]   The legal drinking age in Puerto Rico is eighteen.

ence other places, other cities, other countries. I would like to be in a job where I travel a lot. I would consider returning to Puerto Rico in the future, but it would be during in a phase in my life where I have accomplished what I wished. The only way I can live in Puerto Rico again would be as an adult. I am disappointed in the politics of Puerto Rico, the government. They have lost an entire year on problems that, in the end, don't have a solution. When they do find a solution, it doesn't favor the people. It doesn't matter if it was before the hurricane or after the hurricane. How are we a democratic country if they don't do what the public wants? The people may speak, but the governor will decide differently. I have never voted in Puerto Rico because I don't think any of the people who have run for office can govern Puerto Rico. None of them are convincing. I'm not saying that we need somebody perfect to govern Puerto Rico, but we need someone who is just, which is what Puerto Rico needs. Right now, people who live in public housing practically live better than the middle class. They receive more help, and they don't have to pay as much for things as other people.* It's a lack of respect for others who work. You can work really hard but have no guarantee of being successful in Puerto Rico. You can be the best at what you do, but in Puerto Rico your talent will not be discovered. I don't know if the size of [the] island makes it difficult to stand above the rest, but Puerto Rico is allowing its talent to flee and become talent in other countries. I left, and my college degree will come from here. It would have made me proud for my university degree to come from Puerto Rico because of how difficult it is today to finish the University of Puerto Rico, what with student strikes and the mediocre administration that places more importance on a protest than on your academic progress. We don't have one hundred years of life. We have to take advantage of every minute in our lives. We cannot change the focus of our lives in order to pay more attention to a protest. The students are educating themselves to focus only on problems, and these issues rule your life rather than your goals. We are young. We have fresh energy and should use that energy to be productive. The protests take away our energy, time, and emotions because, if you don't accomplish anything, you get frustrated. What better way to resolve

---

* Public housing residents receive electric rate subsidies and other benefits to which others are not entitled.

our problems than through communication? That's something that Puerto Rico lacks. People don't understand each other, and everybody assumes.

I feel more peaceful here, more independent. I have been able to overcome many obstacles that I wouldn't have faced living under the same roof as my grandmother. I see that everything is possible in life. I see every goal is attainable, as long as you want it. That's my everyday thinking after all that I have experienced. I didn't think that way before. I didn't have such clarity of mind. Before I left Puerto Rico, my perspective was dark. I didn't even know what to do with my life. Once I arrived here and organized my life, I see everything as if it were a satellite map. Everything I want I can achieve. What does a successful person have that I don't have? I have hands and arms and eyes, and we have the same brain. I have no medical condition. So, why can't I achieve my goals? Sometimes people cut off their own wings, saying, "That's not going to work for me." Sometimes we let go of our goals because of other people. If you do what you like, you will be successful. I am sure of it. You shouldn't become too accustomed to things because nothing is permanent. Hurricane Maria clarified my life. It helped me to organize myself, and I learned a lot of things about myself.

José Cruz Vázquez and Yatmarie Negrón Ocasio

Nothing really happened to us.

José Cruz Vázquez, thirty-seven, relocated to Orlando from Las Piedras, Puerto Rico, in April 2018, initially staying with family in Volusia County before finding and preparing an apartment in southeast Orlando for the arrival of his wife Yatmarie Negrón Ocasio, thirty-nine, and daughter Julianna, six years old and a special-needs child. Cruz Vázquez has an MBA and is one of the few post-Maria migrants who requested a job transfer to Florida and therefore had employment waiting for him there. Despite these advantages, Cruz Vázquez and Negrón find themselves lonely and homesick as they adjust for the first time in their lives to a new way of life away from family in Puerto Rico.

[Yatmarie:] Irma was inconvenient—the power went out for three or four days—but it was nothing outside the norm because I survived Hurricane Hugo when I was small, and we survived many days without electricity.

[José:] When they announced that another hurricane was coming, we really didn't pay attention in the beginning. As Maria got closer to Puerto Rico, we understood that we were in greater danger. We began to make different decisions, like picking up things outside the house that could become projectiles and hurt others, protecting our property, autos, and plants. But I tell you, we had no cash on hand when the hurricane arrived. We didn't prepare in that regard.

[Yatmarie:] Nor food. We had no food or maybe food for two weeks. We had water left over from Irma.

[José:] But it was very little. We had what we would normally have in our refrigerator and pantry.

[Yatmarie:] In reality, we didn't prepare as we should have. We collected water because there was a lot of rain, and that helped, but we didn't have enough drinking water. My mom or his mother would give us filtered water to bring back home.

[José:] After the hurricane we realized we should have prepared differently.

[Yatmarie:] We didn't prepare as we should have for the category storm that Maria was projected to be. We felt the force of the hurricane around dawn. At eleven or eleven thirty that night we still had electricity. Then we began to feel the wind go from a little to more and more, and it wouldn't stop.

[José:] Even as we began to feel the winds, we were holed up in our bedroom, the three of us, and the house was hermetically sealed. We heard the wind for six to seven hours.

[Yatmarie:] I asked myself, "My God, when is this going to stop?" We felt uncertain because the wind could break something in the house because our front windows were made of glass.

[José:] We came out of the room now and then because we could see water getting close to the door. We tried to soak up the water coming in through the main door. It was a double door, and the wind was so strong that it separated one door from the other, letting the wind and water seep in.

[Yatmarie:] After we soaked up the water, we rolled a towel and placed it at the bottom of the bedroom door in case the water level rose. It was raining incessantly, and we didn't know exactly where the water was coming from.

José Cruz Vázquez and Yatmarie Negrón Ocasio

[José:] Then the wind changed direction, and the water stopped coming in through the front of the house.

[Yatmarie:] That was about eight in the morning.

[José:] Yes, I left the house about eight in the morning when the wind had died down.

[Yatmarie:] Maybe there was no wind in Las Piedras, but there could have been wind in San Juan. We had only a slight rain.

[José:] We heard a peacefulness that you normally didn't hear. No noise. It was all silence. Other neighbors began coming out too, because the storm had destroyed their main doors or the garage doors.

[Yatmarie:] We began picking up debris and helping each other.

[José:] We had already cleaned up the inside of the house where it had gotten wet. Very little water had come in.

[Yatmarie:] Only in the living room. Nothing really happened to us.

[José:] When we finished helping each other, we began going up on the roofs to remove leaves and other debris. Then we started looking at the main roads to see if we could get out. There were a lot of wood posts and electric wires on the ground. When it began to get dark there was nothing.

[Yatmarie:] No water or electricity or telephone service. We were a little afraid to go out on the main road not knowing what danger lurked there, plus the road was impassable. There were so many downed trees that it was humanly impossible to remove them. We had to wait for machinery to arrive to clean up.

[José:] So the first day after the storm we stayed in the neighborhood and in our home. The second day was the same. I think I returned to work on the fourth day.

[Yatmarie:] A friend came to the house to find out how we made out, and that's how we knew the roads were open. We visited our parents in Las Piedras and Naguabo.

[José:] That day we drove on various roads to get to our parents, and we even made it to Ceiba to retrieve one of our cars, which we had left at her sister's house. We were surprised by the total destruction we saw from Las Piedras to Ceiba. The Walmart in Humacao was totally destroyed. It lost its roof. There was a lot of flooding.

[Yatmarie:] All the stores in that area were destroyed.

[José:] I heard a Walmart marketing person say on the radio that the company was going to invest $10 million to reopen the store. In other words, what we saw between Las Piedras and Ceiba was total destruction. The forests looked as if there had been a fire.

[Yatmarie:] It looked totally burned. Where I am from in Naguabo some of the area is part of El Yunque National Forest. It was green, but it had turned brown. When we saw our parents, they were okay. My mother was a little shaken, but they were alive, which is the most important thing.

[José:] My parents were fine. I thought that the house might have suffered damages since it was built in the 1980s, but the Miami windows had no damage. Maybe a little water came in, but nothing major. When I went back to my job in San Lorenzo—I work in finance—I'd say that's what kept us alive. I could recharge the cell phone, although there was no way to call anyone. I'd recharge my daughter's iPad. I could eat, bring ice back to the house, fill the cars with gas. And it was the only way I could find out what was going on in the island because a lot of workers from all over Puerto Rico would come to the office. That's how we found out what was happening on the western, or southern, or northern areas of the island. I tell you, that's what kept me distracted or entertained.

[Yatmarie:] I was a contract worker for a manufacturing company, and I was not called back to work. I was without work for a month or so. I was alone at home with our daughter waiting for him to arrive, trying to keep her entertained. One day the three of us left to find an ATM machine.

[José:] The day before the hurricane we went to an ATM machine and took out one hundred dollars, which was really nothing since we spent it very quickly.

[Yatmarie:] We had to buy gas for you to go to work.

[José:] I had the luck to mention to my mother that we were essentially without cash, and she had a friend who gave her three hundred dollars to hand to me. I returned the money when I was able to withdraw funds from the bank. I tried to thank him personally on several occasions, but he had a lot of work. I was never able to meet him. That three hundred dollars helped us buy food, what little there was, for several weeks.

[Yatmarie:] We were never able to return to our normal lives after the hurricane. First, we were without drinking water for a month. While my daughter was in school in Naguago, I stayed with my mom and washed clothes by hand.

I'd return home before dark. You didn't know who would be outside after dark. We heard that people were getting robbed, although not in our neighborhood. The power didn't return until November 30, 2017. We used our generator only at certain times, more for our daughter because we're adults and we can survive. Not like our neighbors, who had generators going all the time to power their fans. I couldn't stand in a line for five hours with my daughter just to buy a piece of chicken. I wasn't going on that mission, as we say in Puerto Rico. We ate a lot of canned food. That was the most complicated and difficult thing: to find food.

[José:] When I went to work in the morning I would look for an open supermarket to buy basics, things that couldn't go bad because there was no refrigeration. There was very little merchandise, hardly any water. There were very few businesses open to find food.

[Yatmarie:] I would give him a food list, or my mother in Naguabo would help. We got drinking water through his job, and that was a great help.

[José:] We spent several weeks surviving on what we had in the pantry. We lost weight very quickly. I was stressed out for many days. We slept in the living room because the bedroom was too hot. We heard a lot of noise from generators, plus news reports said that robbers were stealing generators from houses. That created a lot of stress for me, and I couldn't sleep.

[Yatmarie:] The heat also was very strong, and that kept us awake. Even though our house usually is cool, it was very uncomfortable. We spent the hours talking. He would bring home stories from his job, and I would bring home stories about the things I heard in Naguabo, where I was raised. When I began working again, I'd relate stories about my job. Our daughter fell asleep early so we had no choice but to go to sleep too because there was nothing to do.

[José:] We didn't play dominoes or anything like that. Once darkness came, we wouldn't go back outside. We stayed in the house. To stay cool, I bought these little fans, about five inches, that run on batteries or USB. I would charge the fans at work and bring them back home at night. We were able to sleep the entire night with the fans going.

[Yatmarie:] After the hurricane everything slowed down or was delayed. Government offices were closed. Hardly any help arrived where we lived. My mother could get food where she lived and would give some to us. He became an expert in military rations.

[José:] The food is good. You can eat it.

[Yatmarie:] If we had a choice between canned ham and military rations, he would take the military rations. It's more complete.

[José:] My father is [the] owner of a small business, a humble business. He owns a funeral home in Aguas Buenas. His expertise is in finance. He couldn't get to his business for several days. There wasn't enough gasoline to try to get to his job. There was no way for people to contact him by phone.

[Yatmarie:] We only learned recently that there were more deaths. But the funeral directors, among themselves, commented on the deaths. My father-in-law heard, "Over here, a person died for lack of gasoline or lack of dialysis." But the number of deaths wasn't known when the hurricane hit. He is in agreement that the number of deaths was not normal. There was a newspaper report out of Juncos that they registered as many deaths in one day as they normally would in a month. So it was real. People were dying because there was no electricity, no food, especially if you depend on certain foods. Or maybe they ate something that produced an allergic reaction. The grandmother of a friend of my husband's died suddenly of a heart attack. There was no way to get her to a hospital. Hospitals weren't functioning. These are things that were not a direct hit from the hurricane, but people died as a consequence of the storm.

[José:] In a conversation I once had with my father about the subject he said there was an increase in deaths that was not normal when compared with previous months.

[Yatmarie:] Even today there is news of bodies at the Institute of Forensic Science that haven't been claimed.[7] I've never worked for the government, but there were a lot of things that slipped through its hands. I think it could have been better managed.

[José:] I would not have liked to have been in the shoes of any of the people making those decisions. I think I might have retired. This was something on a different level.

We began to hear heartbreaking stories on the news, indicating to us that desperation had arrived. That's when I sat down at my work computer and bought three airfares for Orlando for December to spend a few normal days. We also planned visits to places we were interested in relocating to at some point. We came here to get out of the desperate situation we were in, to be able to take a normal shower, to eat as we had once before, and to relax a little bit.

[Yatmarie:] The last time I was in Florida was in 2000, but it was almost like coming here for the first time because I didn't remember much. We stayed a week with my aunt in Volusia.

[José:] I had never been here before. My company has a manufacturing plant in Orlando, and I paid it a visit, which also was part of the plan, in addition to visiting [the] Magic Kingdom.

[Yatmarie:] His company said to him, "José, whenever you want to move . . ." God had something in store for us. We visited a lot of places to determine whether it was really worth it to move here. When he got the company response, we started to make plans for the move.

[José:] We started to prepare ourselves to move here permanently. Our daughter needs a different kind of education. In Puerto Rico she got a lot of help, a lot of therapy, and we decided to come here and try something different in terms of her education.

[Yatmarie:] Our daughter wasn't able to receive her therapy through the Education Department for a long time. If you don't give special-needs children their therapy, they regress. That was the major reason for leaving. As adults, we had made the best decisions we could to survive the hurricane. She's a child. We wanted her to have something better.

[José:] I tell you, I arrived on April 25 to Jacksonville, and on April 26 my car arrived at the port. I drove to Volusia, where I was staying with her aunt. I tried to look for an apartment or townhouse to rent. On weekends, if I wasn't looking for an apartment to rent, I was washing my car. I would do a little exercise, run a little. I visited a few entertainment places, but I tried not to spend too much money or eat into our budget by doing things that weren't important. I returned to Puerto Rico in May 2018 to visit for a weekend. I decided to rent in this area because of the school, which has a good rating. I wanted my daughter to attend a school with a good rating. This area also was more economical because rents are very high in Orlando.

[Yatmarie:] I am not able to work full-time because I'm with our daughter.

[José:] I moved in on May 30. The rent we pay is double that of our mortgage in Puerto Rico for one-quarter the size of our house.

[Yatmarie:] We rented out our house in Puerto Rico. I arrived on July 20.

[José:] Until she arrived, I had more time to wash the car, do exercise, and discover places that were free. Sometimes I took photographs of lakes and nature to pass the time. I don't have any of the hobbies I had in Puerto Rico. I gave them all up. In Puerto Rico, I had many of the toys that adults have. I used to play paintball, but now I don't have the equipment. I came here with three things: a bag with my camera and electronics, a suitcase with a few clothes, and my car. I didn't bring anything else. I had to give up all my hobbies, and that has been different for me. I don't have friends.

[Yatmarie:] We are starting anew.

[José:] I don't have somebody I can call and say, "Meet me someplace so we can take photos of some place." In Puerto Rico, we'd go to the beach on weekends, or I'd spend time with friends from work. Here we are stepping into new territory. I have the luck to be able to go to work, spend time with coworkers, and be distracted. I talk with my coworkers, and I don't feel alone when I am working. Before she came, I felt very alone. The only other person I had was her aunt. But, in reality, there are only three of us in Orlando. There is nobody else.

[Yatmarie:] I still don't know anyone at my daughter's school. The schools are very different from Puerto Rico. I have to leave her at the door: "Adiós, Julianna." I know where her classroom is, but I don't know what she does in the classroom. In Puerto Rico, I could go into the classroom and speak with the teacher. It's not that you can't do that here, but it's more private. Now I am learning English in the mornings from Monday through Friday, and I am able to pass the time a little. I've met people from China, Brazil, Vietnam, Mexico, Colombia—almost all are Latinos, but from farther away there is a Muslim woman, from Pakistan, I think. In terms of making friends, we are homebodies. We are always together. We're not the type to say, "Let's pass by here on Friday." We have our girl, and also we were never like that. We have not been able to integrate ourselves well in our new place. I feel alone sometimes, but it's because I would go to Naguabo to visit my mom and say: "What are you up to? What have you cooked?" I can't do that now, so in that sense I feel alone. But not for anything else because we are together.

[José:] I think there are a lot of Latinos in Orlando because I hear a lot of Spanish everywhere I go. But beyond getting to know my coworkers, I don't know a lot of people. Most of my coworkers are Puerto Rican. My job is forty-five minutes from here. It could be a shorter commute, but I avoid the tolls, which are expensive. If I take the toll road, I can arrive in twenty-five minutes.

When I lived with Yatmarie's aunt in Orange City it took me an hour and fifteen minutes.

[Yatmarie:] The English you learn in Puerto Rico is very simple. If you don't practice, you will forget it.

[José:] My immediate goal is to dominate the language, to learn English. I cannot say that I'm completely bilingual, but I can defend myself. I'm not going to starve. I want her to feel more comfortable and secure.

[Yatmarie:] We don't really have long-term plans. Our goal is for our daughter to benefit from being here. We think of her first. We're in the process of getting her the same therapy she had in Puerto Rico. Once we accomplish that, I can look for work that complements her schedule.

[José:] Maybe we can return to Puerto Rico someday when our daughter is an independent adult. In the short term, though, I don't think it's possible to return to Puerto Rico. Unfortunately.

[Yatmarie:] I've been here just a month, and I'm not used to it yet. It's not bad here. It's just that the way we were brought up . . . how can I explain? Everyone here is in their home, and everything is closed up. In Puerto Rico I heard more people and the *coquís* [tree frogs] that sang to me by the window every day. You can't even hear the crickets here. We lived ten minutes from his parents' place. If we wanted to see our parents, we'd get in the car and see our parents. I can't do that here. But, like I said, I've been here a month, and I can't say I'm accustomed to it.

I met someone who came in October [2017], and she said she doesn't want to return to Puerto Rico. She goes for a visit and is crazy to return because the quality of life she found here is totally different from the one she left behind. Could you believe we got electricity in Naguabo in May [2018]? May! Everything became more complicated in Puerto Rico. You have to live where you can live best, always remembering family and family unity. It's all about family.

5

THE VIEW FROM ORLANDO

Jorge Olivero Pagán

We survived daily.

Jorge Olivero Pagán, thirty, is originally from Barceloneta, Puerto Rico, and had been living in Orlando for nearly nineteen years when Hurricane Maria struck. He invited all six members of his immediate family—his mother, Jeanette Pagán, forty-six; grandmother Neidis Laureano, seventy-eight; brother Abdiel Olivero, twenty-six; sister-in-law Christina, twenty-five; and three-year-old niece, Sofía, who has autism— to join him in Orlando until things returned to normal on the island. Occasionally, an Orlando-based brother would join them, for a total of six people with Olivero Pagán, a restaurant worker. The family from the island arrived two weeks after the tempest to share a 722-square-foot apartment for seven months. People like Jorge Olivero Pagán represent thousands of Puerto Ricans in Florida and elsewhere who took in family members, sheltering them from further deprivation and trauma.

I am a "Florican," as people like to say. I'm a Floridian and a Puerto Rican, and I've been in Orlando a little longer than I lived in Puerto Rico. Although Puerto Rico will always be my home, I feel very close to home here in Orlando. When we moved to Orlando nineteen years ago, my mother had separated from my father. We were the only ones in the family to move to Florida. At the time of the hurricane, my mother was living in Puerto Rico taking care of my grandmother. You know how it is in Puerto Rico: your grandmother lives here, and a few houses down the road live your aunt, your cousins. That's literally how it is, so my brother lived two houses down from my grandmother. Everybody was living a normal life. Irma came around and didn't really impact Puerto Rico the way Maria did. But when Maria was going to come, they were under the impression that nothing was going to happen, that it's going to be Irma all over again. They weren't ready for Maria, and neither was I.

After Maria hit Puerto Rico I wasn't able to speak with my family for three days or more. One of my main concerns was my grandmother. She is older; she has certain conditions that need to have medical attention on a daily basis, which is one of the reasons my mother was with her. That was one of the scariest parts of it—not knowing how my grandmother was doing and how everybody else was doing, because there was no communication. My grandmother is seventy-eight years old, and she, by the way, takes care of her mother, who is ninety-eight years old and has dementia. My grandmother has to be there daily, and my aunts also help. Not being able to communicate with them after seeing the hurricane on TV, in the newspapers, on the radio were huge concerns. How were they? Were they alive or no? The damage we had seen would make any family member go insane not knowing if they are okay or not. My mother was able to get into a car and drive almost an hour and a half from Barceloneta toward Bayamón or San Juan, where they found a mountainside filled with people who had found a spot with a cellular signal. She said they were driving on the highway, and there were so many trees and stuff you had to drive around. She said she was trying to find other people, trying to see how they were doing because there was no form of communication at all. I don't think there was anyone who wasn't devastated or anxious. When she saw the people gathered, she told my cousin: "Go over there. Those people have to be there for a reason. Look, they have their cell phones out." When I first talked to her, there was relief but also desperation in her tone. She said, "We're not doing okay, but I also don't want to kill you by telling you now that we're not doing okay. Jorgie, what you guys see on the TV is nothing compared to what we have

Jorge Olivero Pagán

lived for the past three days. It doesn't do it justice. You have to be here." I
could remember saying: "Mom, it's going to be okay; things are going to get
better. Hold on tight." But then two or three days would go by, and nothing
changed. Things worsened. The next time I was able to talk with her she said
she was driving toward the beach to gather gallons of water to be able to
flush the toilet, to try to have a normal way of living, but it wasn't working.
We do what we can. We are a very strong race. *La raza latina.* We are survivors. For us, every day is based on our limitations and how much we have to
fight. We survive daily. I knew she would be okay, but she wouldn't be good.
Here in the United States we're lucky. We still have our power, we're still
able to communicate. We had things that they didn't have and they weren't

going to have until . . . when? I went to sleep many nights wondering: "How can I go to sleep okay? Are they okay? Has anyone broken into the house?" This opened up the door to a lot of things that no one was ready for. I was feeling desperation. I was feeling powerless, a feeling of not being able to do something. As much as I wanted to, I couldn't.

I started thinking about bringing them over whenever my mother made trips to the beach for water. I was also hearing that my grandmother was running out of medicine. It was also knowing that my niece, who was three years old—she just turned four—was diagnosed with autism. Sofía is a girl who needs to have therapy on a weekly basis. She is a baby. Unless we take action when she's young, we can't help her to develop the way a normal human being can who doesn't suffer from autism. How can I allow my niece not to have the progress that she needs by just sitting and hoping that things would get better? What can I do? I continue to work because I have all my responsibilities here. As much as I wanted to leave everything that I have here and go over there, I couldn't. Financially, I couldn't. If I were able to go to Puerto Rico, how could I bring over other family members? If I were to do that, I would be jeopardizing what I have and what I can offer if they were to move here. So, I presented the idea to my mother. I said, "Mom, I don't have much money to give you guys. I can't send you guys packages right now. The most that I can do is offer you my home. From here we can rise up again. This might be a new opportunity for us and for us to be together again. Leave that behind and move forward. That's how I feel that I can help." She started crying. She didn't want to take away my privacy, my home, my comfort zone. As a mother she didn't want to do that, but as a son I understood that that's the way a mother would react. She won't ask to move in with me. It's my duty to present it to her, to give her the opportunity to rise up again, like she did when I was young.

When we moved to Florida, we had nothing. She worked three jobs, put us through school to make us the young men that we are today. She gave me that. How can I turn my back on her, my grandmother, my niece, my brother? No. By October 1, they were here. My youngest brother is a pastor in Puerto Rico, and they donated an offering to help him and his family. He, his wife, and daughter were able to come over, while I covered my mother's and grandmother's airfares. My brother is only twenty-six years old, but the work he has done is amazing. For his church and his community to be able to come together and help him, that spoke volumes. God works in mysterious ways. We were able to buy the tickets, which ended up canceled because flights weren't leaving Puerto Rico. The airports were filled with people who had been there for days without power, without water, without food. When my family arrived at the San Juan airport, thank God, I don't know how but they were able to get on the first flight that left. I'd like to give a shout-out to JetBlue. They were amazing in Puerto Rico with all those people. Once over here, as they say in my family, "Where you fit one plate you can fit two or three more," okay? If there's space, we can manage. In my room there was me and my grandmother, and we pushed a bed to the side to fit another queen bed for my sister-in-law and my niece. My family is very united, so my middle brother in Orlando couldn't help himself. He bought a twin-size mattress, and he would sleep in my dining room. He said, "Where there could be six of you guys there could be seven." We hadn't been together for so long. Through the tragedy we found ourselves together again and pushing ourselves. This wasn't going to be the end of us. My family stayed with me up until a month and a half ago.

It broke my heart the way they looked when they arrived. The look on their face said, "We're being strong." But you can see when someone is suffering; you could feel their pain, their energy. Later, they made little comments, like my grandmother would say, "Oh my God, I'm able to have my coffee." There wasn't a day that I would wake up without the smell of coffee in the morning. I love coffee, so that wasn't bad. My mother, Jeanette, would say: "Thank God we were able to go see a doctor. Abuela was running low on blood pressure pills. She can't survive without blood pressure pills." Even being able to turn on the TV and the AC. In Puerto Rico, you have to be very well off financially to be able to afford central AC. My grandmother would say, "Jeanette, I don't even need to dry my sweat." Little things like that made my day. Having food in the fridge for them, knowing that they weren't suffering or having any needs that couldn't be met, pushed me forward. My niece, she can't speak well, but she liked to play. It reminded me of the days I lived in Puerto Rico almost twenty years ago, when I would wake up and my brothers would be within the same four walls, and my grandmother would be having coffee. We were united, and I could see the relief on their faces.

I'm not going to lie. It was very stressful. It came at a time when all of this— my privacy, living alone—I missed that. There was no break. There was always someone here, or more than one person at a time. I didn't really have that moment of silence that I had before, but I couldn't get mad at that because this was the right thing to do. I didn't make the wrong choice. I did what was expected, what I should have done. It came from my heart. I was the one who offered. I had mixed emotions because, damn, I no longer had this place. I live alone for a reason. I work very hard to have this, and I no longer had this. There was a side of me that was not happy with that. I had to control myself, bring myself back down and say, "This too shall pass, and this is what needs to be done." About once a month there would come a moment when I needed my time. Whenever I needed time to myself, I would get in my car, fill up the tank, and drive. I'd drive for hours. No radio, no nothing, just me and my thoughts. I would bring myself back down. I would release whatever I had to release. I gave myself the therapy I needed to bring myself back down. I didn't want to act out with them. They didn't deserve it, and I didn't want to do that. It was me and my own issues. So, I would drive for a few hours, leave my tension, my anxiety, behind. When I returned I was happy. I would open the door, and my niece would run to me and give me a hug. I see my brother is doing better. My grandmother is no longer suffering from losing her medication or any other possibility that could happen. It was no longer a worry. Once we got her to Orlando, we made sure to take her to the Social Security office and transfer everything over, get her in a medical plan in the United States, connect her with doctors. We were so lucky. The response from people who knew these were Maria refugees who desperately needed help was incredible. Everyone was very helpful and willing to help. That's one thing I noticed: Even though this was a tragedy, it brought many people together. People see all the damage that was done to Puerto Rico and they're helpful. They're willing to help. It's not going to happen overnight. It's going to take a lot of time, but we're seeing progress already.

My brother was able to give his daughter a better life and move on with his marriage. It takes courage to leave everything behind. A lot of people left Puerto Rico, but there's still a lot of people in Puerto Rico who will not leave. I fully respect that. I'm not criticizing that at all. Everyone is different; everyone has their own needs; everyone has a different way of thinking. For him to be able to leave the comfort zone, change his mind around and think differently, being able to accept my offer and come, that's a hell of a victory for him. My brother accomplished so much. He performed services in different churches.

He used the offerings he received to buy generators and take them to Puerto Rico. My brother had luggage filled with bottles of water and food to take back and distribute, especially to the church people who gave him a hand. They knew who they were putting their faith in. They knew he'd come back with more than what he had. That's exactly what he did. He took at least five trips to Puerto Rico between October and mid-December to take supplies: batteries, water, generators. He would leave his wife and daughter in Orlando and go to Puerto Rico to distribute these things. He would get in touch with people and ask: "Where does your father live? In Orocovis, on such and such a street? I'll take a drive up there and ask for him. If I find any news, I'll bring it back to you. Give me your number." Words cannot express. It demonstrated what I already knew: how we are. We saw a side of each other that we knew we had but had not come into play before, how we're willing to go above and beyond. Other people have needs. We're not the only ones who have needs. How can I rise above if I leave the ones who were with me behind? Those are my family's qualities. We weren't voicing that enough. Half of my family is evangelical, and the other half is Catholic. Given those two different worlds, you would think there would be rivalry. No, we're actually very respectful of each other. I would go to a service on Sunday and a Mass on Sunday evening. It was common for us to show acceptance. We were very, very united. My family was very accepting of me growing up gay. Not even on that side did I feel secluded, or feel like I needed to exclude others, or that my pain is different from yours, or that what I'm going through is different from what you're going through. No, I was taught to show sympathy for others. You might be going through something, but other people might be going through something too. If you share a little of yourself, somehow we can get through this together. While my family was here, we even had cookout days. We expressed our love through our food. We may not be doing great financially, but if we can express our love to someone, we will find a way. For Christmas, we wanted to show our appreciation to the people who had shown us love—a friend who brought us food, clothing, and other items. We decided to do a *pastelada*. We made *pasteles*. My grandmother, my mother, myself, my sister-in-law, we all made *pasteles*. It was amazing, like the holidays back home.

My apartment complex never said anything about having so many people in the house, but they had to be aware that this happened to Puerto Rico. Puerto Ricans living in all the states had family in Puerto Rico. They had to bring their family members over. It didn't just happen in Orlando. It happened in Miami. It happened in other states. I'm sure that the companies that rent properties to people like myself, who had to bring over family members, didn't take any action due to the circumstances. It would have been inhumane. Still, we kept the curtains closed. We didn't bother anyone or make noise. We're not the type to make a lot of noise. We're very homey. We were just trying to survive and make it through another month without people finding out. I know there were others in the complex with additional family members. There was someone on the third floor who had two family members move in, and another friend brought over two family members, all in this complex.

In the end, everybody went back to Puerto Rico except my mother. She stayed because my grandmother came here for her medical needs, and now she is healthy. She has to see a doctor only every six months. It was my grandmother's decision to go back. My mother agreed as long as she came back every three to four months to see her doctors. She's an adult, she has her house, and we have to respect that. You know how we are. When we get taken away from our house, our home, from what we are passionate about, it's like a little piece of our heart is taken away from us. That was her. She has her house, her gardening, her cooking, my brother next door, and her mother's house is down the road. She needed that, and luckily for us our town has electricity. It was okay for her to move back. Her health is okay. My brother will still look out for her. My mother stayed because not only does she love Florida—she lived here before—but she found another light, another passion. Also, being honest, going back to Puerto Rico right now is a little backtracking. It pains me to say that, but, yes, we are progressing here. Given the choice, she would much rather be here. In no time at all, she'll be able to help the family if they need financial help or any type of medication. If she were to go back to Puerto Rico, things are a little bit harder over there. They're still recovering. My brother had a job at the Barceloneta outlet mall. All of that is completely destroyed. They told him that he would have his job back in April 2018, but it's already mid-June, and there is no word as to when. My mother runs a hotel property over by Highway 192 in Kissimmee. She lives about twenty-five minutes away from me, but she's actually closer to my job. Sometimes she comes over during my break, or I take her out for a fun day. I take her to lunch. We stay in touch.

I am not at peace with the current hurricane season. The anticipation or uncertainty of not knowing has already hit. You see the reports. We're expecting I think ten hurricanes[*] this season. Of those ten, four will be major hurricanes. Even if they say there's a possibility this won't happen, there's always a possibility that one can happen. The people who were prepared somehow weren't even ready for Maria. I can only imagine if this were to strike a second time. My family is the type that everything is okay. We're doing okay, don't you worry. That's what I'm getting hit with: "We're fine, Jorgie, we're fine. Don't you worry." But I'm like, no. I don't want to wear this mask of everything is okay and then have to take it down when everything is crumbling. I need for us to have a backup plan, at least an exit plan if things were to happen the same as last year. I already told them that my house is open. My doors are open the same as they were before. I would not be okay going to sleep knowing my family is not okay. I cannot sleep. I cannot rest. This year will be worse than before because I already know what they went through. If this were to happen again, I will think only of worse things. I don't want to go through that. At least they have a generator where they didn't before. We need to make people more aware. This isn't the first time Puerto Rico has been hit by a hurricane. For Hurricane Georges,[†] I lived an entire month without electricity. I was younger back then so perhaps my mother and father did things that kept me from suffering the way people have suffered now. Before that there was Hurricane Hugo.[‡] It's Mother Nature. We need to make people more aware, more conscious, and bring resources to people who don't have them. Make sure you're safe. I want people to know that we went through something tragic. But as tragic as that was, that's how beautiful it's going to be as we rise. We will not be defeated. This will not be what terminates Puerto Rico. This will not be the end of Puerto Rico. If anything, it has shown how united we are and how we're willing to recover, reconstruct our island, our paradise. I want people to know that we

---

[*] In July 2018 the University of Colorado Department of Atmospheric Science Tropical Meteorology Project downgraded the forecast to four hurricanes, compared with seven predicted in April 2018, or "below average activity," due to a colder Atlantic and the odds of a weak El Niño (https://tropical.colostate.edu/media/sites/111/2018/07/2018-07.pdf).

[†] Hurricane Georges hit Puerto Rico in 1998 as a Category 3 storm.

[‡] Hugo, a Category 3 storm, slammed Puerto Rico in 1989.

are willing to do that, united. The whole world is trying to help us, and it's beautiful. It saddens me that we have to go through something bad for this to happen. But that's in the past. We're moving forward. We're not going to stop until we've reached the point where we can say Puerto Rico has been restored and is back to being a beautiful, enchanted island.

Father José Rodríguez

I'm not used to seeing my people like that.

Father José Rodríguez, thirty-seven, is the interim vicar at Iglesia Jesús de Nazaret, an Episcopal church in Azalea Park, Orlando, the area where his family settled after migrating to Orlando from Hartford, Connecticut, when he was in the second grade. They caravanned with other families from Hartford, arriving in Orlando on the Fourth of July and settling within a ten-minute drive from each other. Azalea Park is considered the first Puerto Rican barrio in Orlando, an area developed in the 1940s that offered affordable housing to many newcomers, as it still does.[1] Rodríguez was assigned to the church a few weeks before Hurricane Maria. Despite being a part-time priest doing the typical pastoral work of preaching, teaching, funerals, and weddings, Rodríguez is a firsthand witness to the flood of survivors who began arriving in Orlando looking for a place to stay and food to eat. He played an instrumental role in creating the Episcopal Office of Latino Assistance and became a vocal advocate for Hurricane Maria survivors.

This has been the biggest moment of reflection of my life. I'm from Puerto Rico, and as a child I remember the stories of Hurricane Hugo. When you hear of a hurricane hitting Puerto Rico, you think of those big concrete houses with the concrete roofs, and you think, *ah, esto es otro huracán.* [This is just another hurricane.] Power will be down for a few days; you'll call your family to see what's

Father José Rodríguez

going on. But then Maria came, and it hovered over the island for an eternity. People immediately were cut off. Before we knew what had occurred, we knew it was different because we had never been cut off from communicating with people before. That was a first. Then you heard about it on the news, and I've never heard about Puerto Rico so much in the news, let alone English-language news. But you still don't know what really happened. It took me days to connect with family members. Then we got called to the airport for the first few flights that were arriving. It was devastating. I've traveled, so I'm not saying this ignorantly, but it felt like I was in some sort of refugee center. The juxtaposition of that beautiful, sleek, modern airport with the people who were arriving . . . I mean these families were arriving in *chancletas* [slippers], T-shirts, shorts; they had no *maletas* [baggage]. You know how people arrive at the airport with goodies, *postres* [desserts], and every now and then somebody sneaks an avocado past US Agriculture? I saw people with no *maletas*, nothing, and barely clothed. If you know anything about *puertorriqueños*, they get all dressed up to go to the airport, meet their families, and it's a party. But it was literally like the walking dead. They were so sad, man. They were tattered. I'm not used to seeing my people like that. We have a strong people, you know. *Somos orgullosos*. Even when things are tough, we stand proud. Those first few days at the airport, that wasn't my culture. It was people who had been really beaten down. It was horrible.

We saw ambulance after ambulance take people to ORMC [Orlando Regional Medical Center] or Florida Hospital. In the first few days Catholic Relief Services set up some doctors, but for some reasons the doctors had to leave. But there was a straight connection of ambulances, medical transport, and taxis taking people who were arriving straight to hospitals. We were there as a church, and one of our first missions was to provide pastoral care. This person is at this hospital, we're going to go visit. That person is at that hospital, we're going to go visit. We were just visiting people at the hospitals and praying with them before we started getting into taking care of physical needs. We realized these are humanitarian flights, women with babies and the elderly. We had elderly coming off the airplanes from Puerto Rico in soiled diapers. We realized we needed adult diapers. If you know anything about our people—I'm going to use the word *orgulloso* again—we don't treat our elderly that way. We saw the desperation on adult children's faces, so we started collecting adult diapers. We saw a lot of trauma. The people arriving were shell-shocked, disoriented, just kind of wandering around. Most of the people I know in Orlando have some family connection here. There is something grounding them. There is a foundation for them here. But most of the families who were arriving didn't have families here. That's kind of weird to say because so many Puerto Ricans have family here, but the ones stuck in FEMA hotels have no other connection. They may have a *primo* or *primo de un primo* [cousin or cousin of a cousin]. There wasn't someone waiting for them at the airport. They just kind of landed in *el mundo del inglés* [the world of English], and many of them had never been to the mainland before. I've been struck by how many families in hotels have never been here before.

Before FEMA started congregating them in Kissimmee, people were staying in hotels along Semoran Boulevard in Orlando. These were the first families that came. Some of them were put on International Drive [tourist district]. How do you service a family on I-Drive? That's been the hardest part for us. FEMA is supposed to be the Federal Emergency Management Agency, but no one had the foresight to place the families near the services they needed. They placed the families wherever FEMA had contracts. I can't service a family on I-Drive, but we did. I can't service a family down Highway 192—it's horrible traffic—but we did. FEMA didn't feel it had [a] duty of care for families they placed in these hotels. They said, "That's not our job." That was said to us in many different ways. Betzy Santiago[2] was a member of our church from Kissimmee. She was in my office with her murderer the Sunday before she was murdered. I was with them, and none of us had any indication that he had those inclinations. It was hard because she was in need, and she was abandoned. She will forever be to me a symbol of abandonment: a strong single mother, a nurse—a nurse!—working a construction job, taking care of her two children and her elderly mother. FEMA cut off aid, and she turns to a friend for help, and that friend did not have her best interests in mind. Why did she have to turn to a friend? Why couldn't she turn to her government? Shouldn't the government have known that these things happen in general? That when people are being cut off from aid on a few hours' notice, they're going to run into the arms of people who don't have their best interests in mind? When you work with vulnerable people you know that vulnerable people have a line of people ready to take advantage of them. Why didn't FEMA have anything in place to protect these vulnerable people? Nothing. Even today, nothing. You would have figured that, with all these people who were going to be homeless, FEMA would have sent someone to go talk with them. FEMA pulled out their caseworkers. The families along 192 were flying alone. No food, no jobs, no transportation. Why in the world would FEMA allow these people to be settled in places that are not conducive to resettlement? Anthropologists who study this subject know that people land in hotels and get trapped there. Have you seen the movie *The Florida Project,* about the stream of motels along Highway 192? Once you get in, you don't get out. The evacuees quickly formed a *barrio.* The Super 8 is a *barrio* for all intents and purposes. They created a community, and that actually made it harder to get them to leave because that was all they had. I would go to the Super 8 and say: "*Mira,* there are apartments in Orlando for eight hundred dollars. Come up to Orlando." And they would say, "No, no, no, I have my *comadre* and *compadre* [friends] here." They watched each other's children. They policed each other. They now had a new safety net, and for me to tell them to come to Orlando, well, they wouldn't. We are a community people. They lost community in Puerto Rico, and they formed community here. They were content, not because they're lazy, but because they didn't want to lose community again. It would retraumatize them. Their children are in schools. They formed community with the school system. They didn't want to retraumatize their children, and they're right. There's no incentive to take your children out of school and move across town to affordable housing. This wasn't thought out very well, not on behalf of families. But there are people who have [a] duty of care to think for them before the survivors got here.

Kissimmee was not conducive to that many families being dumped in a tourist district on the other side of Disney. It's a tourist area where you expect to find touristy things. You don't expect to find things for how to sustain a life. It breaks my heart at how many children live at Disney's back door and have never been to Disney. These hotels are nowhere near fresh food. It's a food desert. The people are chubby because they're eating fast food. We started servicing families through our food pantry. We immediately began putting *productos criollos*—Goya®, *habichuelas* [beans], *arroz* [rice]. We bought brand-new rice cookers. We went out and bought brand-new clothes. It didn't matter what size. People come in all shapes and sizes. In this very room we had tables in a circle, and we stacked bras and panties. Bras were a commodity. People didn't realize the evacuees needed bras. Women were coming from Puerto Rico who didn't have bras. We handed out crates of bras, underwear, and socks. We were approaching winter, so we immediately kicked into a winter drive to get warm clothes for the families. September–October is T-shirt weather for us, but for someone newly arrived [from Puerto Rico] it's cold. We needed to give them some dignity. We got some sweatshirts and were making it up as we went, trying to be as nimble as possible, trying to be unique. From the beginning we wanted to add value. Part of lifting people up is giving them back their dignity, so from the very beginning we wanted to be different. A food pantry with *criollo* products. Clothes pantry with brand-new clothes, clothes that children would actually want to wear. I want the child to walk to school with brand-new clothes, the way all children go to school on the first day. There's nothing wrong with wearing used clothes. I was poor, and I wore used clothes. I was part of the first wave of Puerto Ricans who migrated to the Northeast, and I remember going to pantries, and I remember being grateful for what I received. I just wanted the children to have better. So we made that commitment to be different. We made the commitment to have people actually want to eat our food, for the children to have clothes they wanted to wear, not clothes they were just grateful to have. There's a difference.

The very first day our food pantry opened I wasn't prepared for the shock that the families that I had met at the airport would be the same families to walk through the door. I always remember Debora Oquendo.[3]

I met her at the airport. She was the first mother with a baby in a stroller. I gave her diapers, and I walked away, and she gave them to somebody else. I turned to her, and I said, "Was something wrong? Were they the wrong size? Can I get you something else?" She said, "No, no, *padre*. I have money in my pocket, but that mother didn't. She could use the diapers instead of me." So, I gave her another box of diapers and said, "Promise me you will keep these diapers. These are for you." Then I gave her my cell phone number, and I never saw her again. Then we open the doors, and Reuters is here with us, and she walks in. I didn't recognize her. She said, "*Padre*, it's me, Debora." I looked at her, and all the memories of the airport came rushing back. She looked healthier; she looked fed; she had a few more pounds on her; she looked happy. That was the difference. In that moment she wrapped her arms around me, and we both sobbed right here on this carpet. That day I kept bumping into the families I met at the airport.

We kept the first wave of families that arrived. We didn't let go of those families. Nydia [Irizarry Ramírez; see page 87] was one of those families. Her son was so skinny. They showed up and they had nothing. We didn't let go of them. We didn't know what else to do. These individuals needed help. We couldn't in good conscience, as a church, let them disappear and be forgotten. So we just grabbed onto them. We said, "You stay in connection with us, and we will help lift you up." We did the best we could, one family at a time. One family became ten, became twenty. We have over three hundred families we've directly worked with. About three hundred was our goal, and we exceeded it. We expanded to Kissimmee and worked with hundreds of families, some more closely than others. It's not that we only wanted to help three hundred families, but we only had money to help three hundred families. Once we exceeded three hundred, it became too depressing to track the numbers. It became obvious that we in the church also work paycheck to paycheck. But the key here is, don't abandon families because everyone is abandoning them, everyone is forgetting them. That's where we fit in.

The families that lose their housing vouchers will be retraumatized. We have 140 families, and we think 46 will definitely be homeless. The other 100 families, yes, they have a place to go to, yes, they're going to have a table to eat at, but they're going to lose their community all over again. Children are going to change schools. These children finally have some stability, and now they're being uprooted all over again. The children are definitely worse off than the parents. Children are beginning to exhibit behaviors they never exhibited before. Children are resilient, and when I first met some of them, they were a little bit stunned, but they were happy. At the airport, the parents were the ones who were shell-shocked, and the kids had some life in them. But after eleven months of hotel living, after eleven months of seeing their parents cry, they are not the happy children we first met. The parents are about to get settled in, but the children are completely disconnected. The older ones are acting out, and the younger ones can't process their feelings. Now we have boys who are physically fighting with their parents. They are acting out violently, and parents are saying: "My children never behaved this way. My child has never done this before." I'm hearing that children are having trouble sleeping. The primary effect is from the hurricane, but the secondary effect is the bullying. These kids are getting bullied. They're getting physically attacked. I've called superintendents directly and written letters for parents to school systems, bringing in the weight of the church to state, "My name is Father José, and I'm aware that this is really happening, and I hope you do something about it." And it works, because it scares the school to know that someone else is looking. The community needed mental health to allow them to process their emotions and feelings about what happened. That processing time hasn't happened.

The families who moved to Orlando fared better than the ones in Kissimmee. We have fewer families in hotels in Orlando, and we have more success stories. The families who got here first were able to snatch up the apartments first. The families we served in the first few weeks were able to bounce out of FEMA housing. They grabbed the last bit of affordable housing that we had left in the community. They grabbed the first few jobs. Then we hit a wall. We started to see more people than the economy could absorb, and I think that's what people are forgetting. Even our own brothers and sisters who came earlier from Puerto Rico, they say: "Well, I came from Puerto Rico. I got a job. I'm working. Why can't they do it?" That has been the hardest part. They were the first wave, and the market could absorb them. There were jobs, there were apartments. But, again, communities can't absorb thousands of people. The families in the hotels are up against the fact that there is no housing, there are no jobs. The market has absorbed every person who doesn't speak English that it can. We have to speak of realities. There's only so much that the market will give to a US citizen who doesn't speak English. A job is a job, and every job has its dignity. But a Puerto Rican is not going to take a job that's sub–minimum wage. They say: "I'm not going to work for $2 below the minimum wage, I'm not going to work off the clock, and I'm not going to work ten-hour days. I'm not going to let them treat me as subhuman." This economy is good at using people and throwing them away, but our people know their rights, and that's why they're not getting jobs. The *puertorriqueño* knows his rights. We stand up for each other. That's what I love about our culture. When we see one of our own people beat down, we say "*Anímate, levántate*. I'm going to go fight with you."

Puerto Rico was taken over by an empire in the late 1890s, and we've been trampled by one empire and another. Our people raised themselves up to the point where they say, "Nobody is going to trample us anymore." We know our rights; we know not to allow ourselves to be used. Migrants are not being picky. They know it's not right to be abused. No American, no human being, should take a job where they're going to be abused. Our people were arriving here, and what was being offered to them was practically illegal in some cases. It was subhuman, and we value ourselves more than that. Many families worked these jobs, and they were grateful, but they weren't desperate. There's a difference between being in crisis and being so desperate that you give up the last bit of humanity you have. You've lost everything. All you have is your person. Our people were not willing to give that up. That's why so many people are still in hotels. They're out looking for work, and they've been through many jobs. It's not that they're unemployable. It's that what employers think they can get away with is not happening. They see Puerto Ricans, and they don't realize that we have the same rights as every other American citizen. I'm not justifying paying undocumented workers less, but the reality is the marketplace eats up people. Our workers, sure, they may not speak English well, or they speak it with an accent, but they will not allow themselves to be treated the way other workers are treated here.

We need to reinvest in our community organizations. We're bankrupt, we're cash-flowed out, we're exhausted. We got help from other Episcopal entities that helped fund us, and we also partnered with Vamos4PuertoRico, who brought in some outside money and manpower and helped lift us up. We also worked with the Hispanic Federation, and one of my favorite local organizations was Somos [Proyecto Somos Orlando, part of the Hispanic Federation]. They would bring *quesitos* [pastries] and little Cuban sandwiches. Somos knows how to bring food to the table! We partnered with organizations we felt we could trust. We created the Episcopal Office of Latino Assistance. The reality is the bulk of our efforts were funded by the Episcopal Church, about 80 percent. Collectively, the Episcopal Church has given us about $300,000 in eleven months to help the families. I'd say 90 percent of it went into direct services. We offered microhelp, similar to microlending, drilling down to small needs where we could help with a down payment for a car, auto insurance for six months, an apartment application fee, work boots. I must have bought twenty pairs of skid-proof boots for people with warehouse jobs. We did things to help people lift themselves up. It was based on the honor system. Very few people have burned us. The other 20 percent came from friends. We did have a CEO of a large corporation fly in on a private jet and write a check to help our families, and we were very grateful for it. We helped a lot of families, and we have a beautiful center in Kissimmee on 192 in an old, abandoned rectory that now has a community room, food pantry, pastoral care offices, chapel. We meet the families where they are at. We go back and forth.

Being a church, we have not received the kind of funding we should have. Although we do not evangelize in the spaces we do outreach, we're excluded from a lot of funding sources—government, for instance. A lot of community organizations helped us under the table: "We're giving this to you, but don't tell anyone we gave this to you because we don't give to churches." The community organizations were kind enough to see that we [were] doing something different. Still, no one wants to fund a religious organization. I would respect the government if they had said, "Let us fund you to do this work." Instead they said, "You're in the community, you can do this work well, do the work." There was no mechanism to fund the local church to do this outreach. There was no mechanism to help us help the local community. Our government relied on community organizations to do the work. That was very evident at the airport Resource Center, where about 80 percent of the agencies were community organizations. They were using up their resources to do the government's work. We have spent years spending money out of our reserves, tapping any place we could get money. If we are to help the Puerto Rican masses resettle in central Florida, we need to reinvigorate the organizations so we can continue the work.

We also need to invest in our schools. I don't think that our school system has the cultural competency to understand not only the demographic change, but the cultural change that's going to be happening in the school. These are children that have a beautiful culture, and they do school differently. Their parents relate to the school system differently. The school needs to know that. The school has to provide an education, but nothing says they have to provide it in a certain way other than to meet educational standards. I see the schools grasping at trying to do this. The parents are disconnected from the children's education. That's what we're hearing. There isn't a cultural competency that recognizes a parent reaching out, to want to be part of their child's education, to want to be part of the school community. There's no reciprocating hand in the administration that meets the parents where they are at. We still expect parents to relate to the school system the way the school system is set up. We have to reinvent the way we do schools for the new arrivals. We have to reinvigorate our school organizations. We have to reinvest in them.

We have to look at education, and then we have to look at the job market. Employers have to realize that things are different. It is a right-to-work state, so employers don't have to, but I would like them to. It's the humane thing to do, but, sadly, that's one of the bad parts of being a right-to-work state: employers don't have an obligation to their employees. That doesn't sit well with Puerto Ricans. We believe in mutual obligation. The employer has an obligation to the employee, and, likewise, the employee has an obligation to the employer. We can create a community, a beautiful ecosystem of businesses and communities and people. Here that is broken; it's disjointed because here your employer owes you nothing. That's a very harsh reality for hardworking Puerto Ricans to step into. It says that I can work hard, that I can give my all to my employer, but they don't have to reciprocate. They can get rid of me at a moment's notice. That's the number-one thing I hear in pastoral counseling. They've never been in a situation like that.

We know what we should be doing, and we are gradually moving toward it. We're putting together all our contact information in a database to set up a communication platform so that in one click I can message my members on WhatsApp, Facebook, email, and text messages. I got cut off from the people that I serve[d] during Irma, so we're trying to come up with a better communication plan. Ideally, I would love to have a storehouse with one to two months of food, but we're hand-to-mouth. We need a computer lab with computers, printers, and copiers so families can look for jobs and apartments. That's part of building resiliency. We're working toward that goal, but the reality is, we can't do future hurricane preparedness because we're still in crisis from Maria. How can I plan for the future if I'm still living in the present? We're trying to plan for the future because we can't get caught like this again. We're thinking resiliency. We're thinking ahead. We're praying that partnerships come through for counseling, mental health, and social work needed in the community. We're preparing for the next crisis.

6

CONCLUSION

María T. Padilla

When we sat down to interview the hurricane survivors, we had no idea what to expect. We did not know any of the people beforehand. We did not know their backstory—what island town they came from; what schooling they had; what jobs they held; if they had ever lived in the States; whether they were married or had children; and what happened to them during the hurricane. We knew only that they were survivors of Puerto Rico's Hurricane Maria who had escaped to the Orlando, Florida, area, and we definitely wanted to talk with each. During the course of the interviews, however, certain patterns emerged underscoring pre-Maria Puerto Rican migration trends that scholars and others have previously noted. If a trend exists, random people will reflect it, and the survivors did. Here are some of the patterns uncovered during the interviews.

The clearest and most obvious trend is that Puerto Rican migration to the States accelerated following Hurricane Maria, with a net migration of 77,321 in 2017, up from an average of 65,000 in previous years. The figure may be even higher, according to the Center for Puerto Rican Studies in New York, because of the way a US Census survey defined evacuees, including that they had to have arrived in the States *before* Hurricane Maria swept the island.[1] In

2019 the US Census published new migration numbers, indicating that a total of nearly 130,000 people left Puerto Rico from July 2017 to July 2018, or 4 percent of the island's population, in the year following Hurricane Maria, one of the highest migrations of Puerto Ricans ever recorded in a single year.[2]

Evacuees also preferred Florida, a state that has received, both before and after Hurricane Maria, the largest influx of Puerto Ricans from the island. Florida is now the epicenter of the Puerto Rican migration not just from the island but also from other states where Puerto Ricans have historically settled, particularly in the Northeast. The lower estimate of the post-Maria exodus to Florida is 41,000, with nearly 83,000 representing the upper bound.[3] Florida researchers settled on a figure of 53,000, cited in this book and in various papers.[4] In the 2017 census survey, 29 percent of Puerto Rican migrants settled in Florida, nearly four times as many as the next-closest state, Pennsylvania.[5] In addition, more Puerto Ricans are still drawn to the Orlando area (Orange, Osceola, and Seminole Counties), where 334,143 Puerto Ricans reside—about 100,000 more than in south Florida's most populous counties (Miami-Dade, Broward, and Palm Beach).[6]

From a demographic standpoint, ten of the fifteen interviewees were women, who are increasingly the face of the Puerto Rican migration to Florida. In central Florida, where Puerto Ricans predominate among all Hispanics, Latinas outnumbered Latinos 56 percent to 44 percent before the hurricane. In Orlando the differential is even greater: 59 percent to 41 percent.[7] Many of the evacuee women came with children in tow. Six of the fifteen interviewees migrated with children and in some cases grandchildren, signaling that the well-being of offspring may have been a driving or deciding factor in their migration. A later study showed that 23 percent of Puerto Rican children experienced some form of anxiety after Hurricane Maria, and 31 percent of families with children reported that their socioeconomic conditions deteriorated after the hurricane. In addition, the study noted that children began exhibiting behavioral issues as a result of the storm, including lack of concentration, slow academic progress, and little interest in studying. Conditions such as anxiety, fear, and depression were found among the children of Maria, especially among families who suffered material losses.[8] What's more, a large number of migrants or their loved ones were ill or had prior medical conditions that were exacerbated by the storm. Among six of the fifteen interviewees, they, their spouses, or children experienced medical issues from anxiety, depression, and high blood pressure to heart conditions, stroke, and cancer. At least two of the interviewed evacuees had a special-needs child or a child on the autism spectrum.

As is often the case, educational attainment and occupation mattered in the outcomes for evacuees. The two evacuees who experienced the least financial disruption and made the easiest economic transition to the States had college degrees. One was a teacher, and the other held a master's degree in business administration and arrived in Orlando via a company transfer, underscoring that the social and financial capital that migrants bring with them makes a difference, as does class origin.[9] Those who struggled the most possessed limited capital and/or were sick, ill, or tending to others, affecting their ability to more fully integrate into the economy and culture. However, all survivors took advantage of informal networks of people and information to get ahead, establishing their resourcefulness. This was especially true of the migrants living in hotels who bonded and formed a community among themselves. Others relied on family and friends already living in the Orlando area. This is typical of how Puerto Rican migrants generally conduct themselves to find information and tease a sense of coherence out of their new environment.[10]

After Hurricane Maria, however, the survivors' emotions were deep, raw, and confused, with most directing their ire at Puerto Rico's local and central governments for not doing enough, in their view, to mitigate the disaster pre- and posthurricane or to pull back from a natural and man-made catastrophe that worsened Puerto Rico's economic and demographic undoing. The survivors often posed an unanswerable, existential question to themselves and others for which there is no simple answer: Why did we have to go through this?

For about fifteen Puerto Rican evacuee families, the disaster was duplicated, for they experienced two hurricanes—Maria in Puerto Rico and later Michael in Florida. After fleeing Hurricane Maria for the Florida Panhandle, these fifteen families suffered the wrath of Hurricane Michael, with further devastation and loss, when the Category 5 hurricane sliced across Mexico Beach, Florida, on October 10, 2018, approximately one year after Maria. Familiar complaints of slow federal response and recovery efforts soon emerged.[11]

Two years after Hurricane Maria smacked into Puerto Rico, the aftereffects are still unfolding, with the long-term consequences and impacts still not completely known. Reporting thus far has outlined issues that took an immediate toll on Puerto Rico and its millions of Maria survivors. But the hurricane and its aftermath continue to generate daily news stories; sometimes as many as ten or more arrive in a single day in a Google news alert. That is a good thing because a sense of accountability for the entire hurricane event still is lacking, although it is clear that the local and federal government bear great responsibility for the horrific outcomes. The Puerto Rico government finally completed a natural disaster contingency plan in June 2019, but didn't make it public until August 2019, when Hurricane Dorian threatened the island—that is, two months after the start of the year's hurricane season and two years after Maria. The report, titled *Joint Operational Catastrophe Incident Plan of Puerto Rico,* noted that "it was the first time in the history of Puerto Rico, the government has joined the private sector, and non-governmental sectors to create" a disaster plan.[12] In it, the Puerto Rico government cast blame around but, more importantly, finally conceded that "the federal, state and local governments; the private sector; and the general population were not prepared for an event of such historical consequences."

Later, in July and August 2019, Puerto Ricans pushed back against government officials when protestors took to the streets of San Juan, Puerto Rico, prompted in part by obscene and vulgar revelations contained in private texts known as "#RickyLeaks,"[13] after then governor Ricardo Rosselló, in which close aides had ridiculed the hurricane dead, among other things.[14] The protestors eventually forced Rosselló out of office in what may be the beginning of a ritualistic and political posthurricane purification and cleansing.

It will take years and many more studies for elected officials to come to full terms with the fault lines of Hurricane Maria preparedness and response, specifically the roles they played as government representatives. Unanswered questions include: Where is the accountability for actions during and after Hurricane Maria? Should Puerto Ricans look to the municipalities or the central government for hurricane preparedness and response? Where is the handoff between the Puerto Rico and federal governments in hurricane preparedness and response? Considering that Puerto Rico has been a Spanish-speaking territory of the United States for 121 years, what type of linguistic and cultural competency should be required in federal preparedness and response efforts?

More long-term research is necessary to paint a more accurate portrait of how Puerto Ricans endured and survived such a catastrophic natural—and, important to note, man-made—disaster. Some universities are stepping into the research gap, with the Center for Puerto Rican Studies, part of the City University of New York's Hunter College, leading the way, publishing an ongoing series of research and critical analyses about Hurricane Maria's aftermath, especially how the unprecedented Puerto Rican migration affected stateside communities. The University of Central Florida inaugurated the UCF Puerto Rico Research Hub in 2019, an appropriate move considering that central Florida is now the locus of the Puerto Rican diaspora in the United States. It has collaborated with partners, such as the Center for Puerto Rican Studies, to bring hurricane-related research and information to students, scholars, and the public at large. The University of South Florida and Florida International University have both conducted daylong workshops and discussions on the Puerto Rican migration.

Scholars and others seek to answer the questions affecting Puerto Ricans on this side of the Atlantic:

- How have migrants changed since the hurricane?
- What, if anything, are Puerto Rican migrants doing differently today?
- What has been the hurricane's long-term mental and emotional impact on the migrant population?
- What is the hurricane's continuing effect on migration to Florida and other states?
- How have Puerto Ricans acclimated in Florida, the state receiving the most migration?
- Is the post-Maria settlement a permanent one, or does it continue the previous pattern of circular migration, the so-called "come-and-go" of Puerto Ricans to and from Puerto Rico?

Many questions still demand answers, for the more the surface is scratched, the more questions arise. The public should continue to press for greater government accountability in natural disaster response. After all, these are tax dollars at work—or not. As American people, Puerto Ricans deserve no less.

AFTERWORD

The fierce winds of Hurricane Maria have receded, replaced by the gentler trade winds for which Puerto Rico is known. However, the storm still rages on other fronts as new developments and stories about Maria continue to unfold. The state of the survivors and the recovery of Puerto Rico remains in a constant state of flux. A visit to Puerto Rico mountain towns walloped by Maria made it clear that the island is getting a fresh coat of tropical paint as homeowners and businesses piece together the things that fell apart. Bridges that washed away, such as in Ciales, are being rebuilt. And Puerto Rico, once again, has turned an emerald shade of green. But it's fair to say that Puerto Rico is not "back" yet, as evidenced by downed traffic lights or ones that don't work, damaged utility poles on the roadside, blue tarps on roofs, and even hurricane debris still to be picked up. The big exodus of migrants has subsided somewhat—for now—but many who moved to Florida are still grappling with adjusting to their very different lives in new surroundings. In a Puerto Rican Studies Research Summit at the University of Central Florida in 2019, an Orange County School Board member said the school district had enrolled more than 1,100 Hurricane Maria students of whom 120, or 11 percent, were still homeless.[1] Orange County has the highest population of Puerto Ricans in the central Florida area. Here is a partial update to the stories of the survivors chronicled in *Tossed to the Wind*.

The regreening of the town of Ciales in 2018 signals hope for Puerto Rico. Photo by María T. Padilla.

Two of the survivors interviewed for the book returned home: Sugeilly Meléndez and her daughter, Layla Zoe Martínez Meléndez, as well as Wilda Cirino and her infant son, Lionel. At the time of her interview, Meléndez was waiting to buy return tickets to Puerto Rico, so her departure was no surprise. Cirino, however, spoke adamantly about staying in Florida. Some Baymont Inn residents attributed Cirino's return to Puerto Rico to her father, who they said had fallen ill.

Rosa Then Ortiz's husband, Cruz Then Lorenzo, was hospitalized shortly after the interview, undergoing a hernia operation. He remained in a Polk County hospital for months. The couple was later approved for an affordable apartment in Winter Haven, Polk County, for which they had been on a waiting list. It became apparent that Rosa Then Ortiz wasn't eager to move, fearing she would lose the community of like-minded people who had experienced the same displacement under the same set of circumstances as she had. Family, whether real or improvised, was important to Rosa Then Ortiz, who so lamented leaving the island during her interview. Once FEMA ended the Transitional Sheltering Assistance hotel voucher program, Then Ortiz made the move to Polk County, assisted by her teacher-daughter, who returned to Orlando from Puerto Rico. The daughter was looking for a Florida teaching post, Then Ortiz said at the time.

Things markedly improved for Miriam Echevarría and José Antonio Vázquez, the couple who couldn't agree on whether to stay or return to Puerto Rico. Vázquez was approved for Social Security Disability and the healthcare coverage that comes with it. He subsequently underwent heart surgery and an operation to improve the circulation in his legs, meaning the state of his health was still touch-and-go. Echevarría, meanwhile, worked when she could, including as a housekeeper at the Baymont Inn. The couple was actively searching for an apartment now that their income was more secure.

Dacny Segarra, who came to Florida with thirteen relatives, was proud that all of her children had landed jobs. Still, affordable housing—a manufactured or a single-family home to accommodate the large family—remained out of reach. After the housing vouchers were eliminated, she and her family moved to another hotel.

Nydia Irizarry Ramírez lost an old job and found a new job, in each case helping Hurricane Maria survivors. Rebecca Colón is teaching at a Poinciana elementary school, as she had planned.

Father José Rodríguez continued to advocate for Maria survivors through the Episcopal Office of Latino Assistance and to work with other organizations. He commemorated the one-year anniversary of Hurricane Maria with a special event held at Iglesia Jesús de Nazaret, where he was later appointed permanent vicar. The activity was attended by a number of elected officials and covered by many Orlando news stations. Father Rodríguez is often seen on television advocating on behalf of Maria evacuees. Later, Iglesia Jesús de Nazaret, in conjunction with the University of Central Florida Restores program, opened a mental health clinic at the church for hurricane survivors.[2]

The hotels themselves merit a postscript, for on more than one occasion we arrived at the Baymont Inn or Super 8 in Kissimmee to find the property undergoing extensive renovations and repairs. New paint, new furniture, new mattresses, and more—an indication that the Maria migrants had provided a financial boost to the businesses due to sustained high occupancy rates. FEMA payments flowed directly to hotel owners, not the evacuees. To underscore the point, a *Hotel News Now* analysis showed that FEMA spent more than $480,000 for the Transitional Sheltering Assistance program in Florida after Hurricane Irma, providing a "welcome revenue boost to hotels."[3] Bear in mind that FEMA's hotel housing assistance program after Maria was significantly larger and lasted longer, meaning the impact to the hotels' bottom lines likely was more significant. And not to be overlooked, the Baymont Inn itself changed hands when a Hialeah, Florida, company bought the 130-room property for nearly $4.8 million in June 2018.

Graffiti on a house in Utuado cries out for liberty and justice. Photo by María T. Padilla.

ACKNOWLEDGMENTS

We owe a special thank-you to Dr. Patricia Silver, a friend and mentor, who recommended us for this important project. A debt of gratitude also goes to all of the interviewees who, although apprehensive and maybe even initially suspicious, trusted and honored us with their amazing stories: Dacny Segarra, David Olmeda, Rosa Then Ortiz, Wilda Cirino, Miriam Echevarría and José Antonio Vázquez, Layla Martínez Meléndez, Sugeilly Meléndez, Rebecca Colón, Nydia Irizarry Ramírez, Glorimar Torres, Ivelisse Marrero, Margarita Rodríguez Guzmán, Coralis Alméstica Cintrón, José Cruz Vázquez and Yatmarie Negrón Ocasio, Jorge Olivero Pagán, and Father José Rodríguez. To Stephanye Hunter for encouraging us to tackle the project and then giving us the space to work on it. To TT Publications Inc. for being so accommodating. To the Puerto Rican community of Orlando, which is ever growing, ever changing, ever diverse, and ever fascinating.

NOTES

Chapter 1. A Storm for the Ages

1. "Detailed Meteorological Summary on Hurricane Irma," National Weather Service, National Oceanic and Atmospheric Administration (hereafter NOAA), https://www.weather.gov/tae/Irma_technical_summary. Irma was a Category 5 storm that passed north of Puerto Rico and slammed into Florida.

2. Trevor Houser and Peter Marsters, *The World's Second Largest Blackout,* report, RHG.com, https://rhg.com/research/puerto-rico-hurricane-maria-worlds-second-largest-blackout/.

3. "The Mind-bending and Heart-breaking Economics of Hurricane Maria," Climate Impact Lab, ImpactLab.org, http://www.impactlab.org/news-insights/the-mind-bending-and-heart-breaking-economics-of-hurricane-maria/. Maria was not a "1-in-10 event" or even a 1-in-100 event. Considering both the storm's physics and how it mapped on the Puerto Rican territory, Maria was more like a 1-in-3,000 event.

4. Zora Neale Hurston, *Their Eyes Were Watching God* (Chicago: University of Illinois Press, 1978), 230. In her seminal novel, Hurston described the catastrophic Lake Okeechobee hurricane that hit Florida in 1928.

5. "Major Hurricane Maria," NOAA, Weather.gov, https://www.weather.gov/sju/maria2017.

6. US Census Bureau, Puerto Rico, "Comparative Demographic Estimates, 2017 American Community Survey, 1-Year Estimates," https://factfinder.census.gov/faces/tableservices/jsf/pages/productview.xhtml?pid=ACS_17_1YR_CP05&prodType=table.

7. NOAA, "Major Hurricane Maria."

8. "Hurricanes: Science and Society," University of Rhode Island, hurricane-science.org, https://www.hurricanescience.org/history/storms/1920s/.

9. Sherry Johnson, "The History and Science of Hurricanes in the Greater Caribbean," latinamericanhistory.oxfordre.com, http://latinamericanhistory.oxfordre.com/view/10.1093/acrefore/9780199366439.001.0001/acrefore-9780199366439-e-57.

10. Government of Puerto Rico, *Transformation and Innovation in the Wake of Devastation: An Economic and Disaster Recovery Plan for Puerto Rico*, Report to Congress, July 9, 2018. http://www.p3.pr.gov/assets/pr-transformation-innovation-plan-congressional-submission-080818.pdf. See also Frances Robles, "Puerto Rico Spent 11 Months Turning the Power Back On: They Finally Got to Her," *New York Times*, August 14, 2018.

11. Houser and Marsters, "The World's Second Largest Blackout."

12. Puerto Rico Farm Bureau to Senator Orrin Hatch, "Recommendations from the Puerto Rico Farm Bureau to the Puerto Rico Oversight, Management, and Economic Stability Act (PROMESA) Task Force," senate.gov, https://www.finance.senate.gov/imo/media/doc/Puerto%20Rico%20Farm%20Bureau.pdf.

13. Government of Puerto Rico, *Transformation and Innovation in the Wake of Devastation*, 16, 17. People over age sixty make up 25 percent of Puerto Rico's population, the highest ratio in the region, including Florida, where 21 percent of the population is over sixty.

14. Omayra Sosa, "Se disparan en casi mil las muertes tras Maria," periodismoinvestigativo.com, http://periodismoinvestigativo.com/2017/12/se-disparan-en-casi-mil-las-muertes-tras-maria/. Sosa's study was based on numbers provided by the island's Demographic Registry. For an English-language version of the study, see Omayra Sosa and Julio Ricardo Varela, "Nearly 1,000 More People Died in Puerto Rico after Hurricane Maria," latinousa.org, https://latinousa.org/2017/12/07/nearly-1000-people-died-puerto-rico-hurricane-maria/.

15. Nishant Kishore, Domingo Marqués, Ayesha Mahmud, et al., "Mortality in Puerto Rico after Hurricane Maria," *New England Journal of Medicine*, Special Report 379, May 2018, 162–70, https://www.nejm.org/doi/10.1056/NEJMsa1803972. This analysis was based on a randomized survey of 3,299 households from January 17 through February 24, 2018.

16. George Washington University, Milken Institute of Public Health, *Ascertainment of the Estimated Excess Mortality from Hurricane Maria in Puerto Rico*, August 2018, p. 4, pdf, https://publichealth.gwu.edu/sites/default/files/downloads/projects/PRstudy/Acertainment%20of%20the%20Estimated%20Excess%20Mortality%20from%20Hurricane%20Maria%20in%20Puerto%20Rico.pdf.

17. Government of Puerto Rico, *Transformation and Innovation in the Wake of Devastation*, 28.

18. US Congress, *Congressional Task Force on Economic Growth in Puerto Rico: Re-*

port to the House and Senate, 114th Cong., Congressional Report, December 2016, 17, 18. The report indicates that under Medicaid, for instance, Puerto Rico's funding is capped each year, compared with the open-ended funding for the fifty states and the District of Columbia, among other differences. Puerto Rico also is not included under Supplemental Social Security Income for the poor, but if it were included it could receive nearly $2 billion annually (pp. 52–54).

19. "Plebiscito para la descolonización inmediata de Puerto Rico, Escrutinio," ceepur.org, http://resultados2017.ceepur.org/Escrutinio_General_79/index.html#es/default/CONSULTA_DE_ESTATUS_Resumen.xml. Only 23 percent of eligible voters participated, the lowest turnout in Puerto Rico electoral history. Nonbinding political status plebiscites were also held in 1967, 1993, 1998, and 2012.

20. Juan R. Torruela, "The Insular Cases: A Declaration of Their Bankruptcy and My Harvard Pronouncement," in *Reconsidering the Insular Cases, the Past and Future of the American Empire,* ed. Gerald L. Neuman, 61–76 (Boston: Harvard University Press, 2015).

21. Jorge Trías Monge, *The Trials of the Oldest Colony in the World* (New Haven: Yale University Press, 1997). Trías Monge is also a former chief justice of the Puerto Rico Supreme Court.

22. "U.S. Citizenship in Puerto Rico: One Hundred Years after the Jones Act," ed. Edwin Meléndez, special issue, *CENTRO: Journal of the Center for Puerto Rican Studies* 29, no. 1 (2017): 4.

23. Charles Venator-Santiago, "Today, Being Born in the Puerto Rico Is Tantamount to Being Born in the United States," in "U.S. Citizenship in Puerto Rico: One Hundred Years after the Jones Act," special issue, *CENTRO: Journal of the Center for Puerto Rican Studies* 29, no. 1 (2017): 15.

24. Landmark United States civil rights cases, https://www.senate.gov/artandhistory/history/common/generic/CivilWarAmendments.htm.

25. Juan R. Torruela, "The Insular Cases: The Establishment of a Regime of Political Apartheid," 29 U. Pa. J. Int'l L. 283 (2007).

26. Anthony Scalia, Hamdan v. Rumsfeld, 548 U.S. 557 (2006), JUSTIA: U.S. Supreme Court, 2006, at 9. https://supreme.justia.com/cases/federal/us/548/557/. In his dissent to the Guantánamo case, *Hamdan vs. Rumsfeld* (2006), Scalia wrote: "[I]t is clear that Guantanamo Bay, Cuba, is outside the sovereign 'territorial jurisdiction' of the United States. . . . Petitioner, an enemy alien detained abroad, has no rights under the Suspension Clause."

27. Puerto Rico Planning Board, *Statistical Appendix of the Economic Report to the Governor and to the Legislative Assembly*, 2017. For economic activity, see "Table 1, Selected Series of Income and Product, total and Per Capita."

28. Bipartisan Congressional Task Force on Economic Growth in Puerto Rico, *Report to the House and Senate,* December 20, 2016, 12.

29. Michael Corkery and Mary Williams Walsh, "Puerto Rico's Governor Says

Island's Debt Is 'Not Payable,'" *New York Times*, June 28, 2015. Then governor Alejandro García Padilla made a more public statement in a televised address to the island a day later. The next year, the US Supreme Court denied Puerto Rico's bid for bankruptcy, stating that the island "misread" the bankruptcy code, which doesn't give Puerto Rico the authority to take advantage of debt relief provisions available to the fifty states. See also Jess Bravin, "Supreme Court Strikes down Puerto Rico Debt-Restructuring Law," *Wall Street Journal*, June 13, 2016.

30. Mary Williams Walsh, "Puerto Rico Declares a Form of Bankruptcy," *New York Times*, May 3, 2017.

31. Stuart B. Schwartz, "Puerto Rico's Hurricane Maria Proves Once Again That Natural Disasters Are Never Natural," October 2, 2017, historynewsnetwork.org, https://historynewsnetwork.org/article/167090. Schwartz's examination of Hurricane San Ciriaco is considered the first to connect a hurricane event with political process. See Stuart B. Schwartz, "The Hurricane of San Ciriaco: Disaster, Politics, and Society in Puerto Rico, 1899–1901," *Hispanic American Historical Review* 72, no. 3 (August 1991): 320.

32. Puerto Rico Planning Board, "Statistical Appendix of the Economic Report to the Governor 2017," table 34.

33. US Senate, Testimony of Ricardo Ramos before the Senate Energy and Natural Resources Committee, November 2017, c-span.org, https://www.c-span.org/video/?c4691769/ricardo-ramos-en-el-senado. Ricardo Ramos, former head of PREPA, testified: "It's very hard to manage PREPA, being a big corporation and part of government. Even in its current bankruptcy, PREPA is like the jewel of the crown of Puerto Rico, regardless of the bad service and the bad condition it is in. Certainly there is too much intervention by government officials. . . . PREPA traditionally has been a company where politicians or parts of government can get their family members to get work. Percentage-wise certainly over 50 percent [of employees]. Historically, PREPA has served as the place for employment for families of political figures since the 70s."

34. George Washington University, Milken Institute of Public Health, *Ascertainment of Excess Mortality*, pdf, pp. 39–40.

35. George Washington University, Milken Institute of Public Health, *Ascertainment of Excess Mortality*, pdf, 41.

36. Government Accounting Office (hereafter GAO), *2017 Hurricanes and Wildfires, Initial Observations on the Federal Response and Key Recovery Challenges, September 2018*, 28.

37. GAO, *2017 Hurricanes and Wildfires*, 36.

38. Federal Emergency Management Agency (hereafter FEMA), *2017 Hurricane Season FEMA After-Action Report*, July 2018, 16, 17, 20.

39. GAO, *2017 Hurricanes and Wildfires*, 37. In addition, the Census Bureau stated in a memo dated May 16, 2018, that it made a major program decision to conduct

an "update-leave" operation in all of Puerto Rico, not just in specific areas, to verify and update addresses during the 2020 census.

40. GAO, *2017 Hurricanes and Wildfires*, 31.

41. C. E. Willison, P. M. Singer, M. S. Creary, et al., "Quantifying Inequities in U.S. Federal Response to Hurricane Disaster in Texas and Florida Compared with Puerto Rico," *BMJ Global Health* 2019; 4:e00191, p. 2, https://gh.bmj.com/content/4/1/e001191.

42. Williston, Singer, Creary, et al., "Quantifying Inequities," 4.

43. GAO, *2017 Hurricanes and Wildfires*, table 1, 46.

44. FEMA, *2017 Hurricane Season FEMA After-Action Report*, 41. "In Puerto Rico, the Territory [*sic*], requested that FEMA activate TSA on October 25, more than a month after landfall. FEMA approved the request three days later."

45. FEMA, *2017 Hurricane Season FEMA After-Action Report*, appendix A-2.

46. Jorge Duany, *The Puerto Rican Nation on the Move: Identities on the Island and in the United States* (Chapel Hill: University of North Carolina Press, 2002), 67-68.

47. Nelson Denis, *War Against All Puerto Ricans* (New York: Nation Books, 2015), 29.

48. Schwartz, "The Hurricane of San Ciriaco."

49. Gabriel Stargardter and Dave Graham, "Trump Lays Blame on Puerto Ricans for Slow Hurricane Response," *Reuters*, September 30, 2017, https://www.reuters.com/article/us-usa-puertorico-trump/trump-lays-blame-on-puerto-ricans-for-slow-hurricane-response-idUSKCN1C50GQ.

50. David Nakamura, "'It Totally Belittled the Moment': Many Look Back in Dismay at Trump's Tossing of Paper Towels in Puerto Rico," *Washington Post*, September 13, 2018.

51. Eileen Sullivan, Julie Hirschfeld Davis, and Nicholas Fandos, "Trump Denies Puerto Rico Death Toll, Falsely Accusing Democrats of Inflating the Numbers," *New York Times*, September 13, 2018.

52. Annie Karni and Patricia Mazzei, "Trump Lashes Out Again at Puerto Rico, Bewildering the Island," *New York Times*, April 2, 2019.

53. Katie Zezima, "Puerto Rico Pushes for Statehood, Calling It a Civil Rights Issue," *Washington Post*, June 27, 2018.

54. María T. Padilla, "The Push for Puerto Rico Statehood," March 29, 2019, orlandolatino.org, http://orlandolatino.org/2019/03/puerto-rico-statehood/.

55. GAO, *2017 Hurricanes and Wildfires*, 26.

56. Government of Puerto Rico, *Transformation and Innovation in the Wake of Devastation*, 12.

57. History Task Force, *Labor Migration under Capitalism: The Puerto Rican Experience* (New York: Center for Puerto Rican Studies, City University of New York, 1979), 15.

58. Kurt Birson, "Puerto Rican Migration and the Brain Drain Dilemma," in *Puerto Ricans at the Dawn of the New Millennium*, ed. Edwin Meléndez and Carlos Vargas-Ramos (New York: Center for Puerto Rican Studies, City University of New York, 2014), 4.

59. US Census Bureau, Population Division, "Annual Estimates of the Resident Population," April 2019. To be exact, Puerto Rico lost 129,848 people by July 2018, or 4 percent of its population in the year following Hurricane Maria, one of the largest population declines ever recorded.

60. Edwin Meléndez, "Upwards of 175,000 People Have Fled Puerto Rico in the Year since Hurricane Maria," press release by Carlos Vargas-Ramos, Center for Puerto Rican Studies, City University of New York, September 2018.

61. Comité Multisectorial para el Reto Demográfico, "Resumen del informe de progreso: Acercamiento a problemas y soluciones," June 2018, 2.

62. María T. Padilla, "Hurricane Maria Galvanizes Puerto Ricans in Central Florida," orlandolatino.org, September 22, 2017, http://orlandolatino.org/2017/09/hurricane-maria/. See also María T. Padilla, "Hurricane Supplies May Go to Waste," orlandolatino.org, February 10, 2018; and http://orlandolatino.org/2018/02/hurricane-supplies/. Many supplies collected had to be given away locally after organizations had no way of getting material to Puerto Rico, while other supplies never made it to Puerto Rico, instead rotting in storage, a problem that also cropped up in Puerto Rico.

63. Jorge Duany, "The Orlando Ricans: Overlapping Identity Discourses among Middle-Class Puerto Rican Immigrants," *CENTRO: Journal of the Center for Puerto Rican Studies* 22, no. 1 (Spring 2010): 87.

64. Patricia Silver, "Puerto Ricans in Florida," in *Puerto Ricans in the New Millennium*, ed. Meléndez and Vargas-Ramos, 72.

65. One-year estimate, American Community Survey, 2017, US Census: https://factfinder.census.gov/faces/tableservices/jsf/pages/productview.xhtml?pid=ACS_17_1YR_B03001&prodType=table. Survey represents pre-Maria figures with the Cuban population at 1,528,046 versus 1,128,225 for Puerto Ricans.

66. Florida Legislature Office of Economic and Demographic Research, *Florida: An Economic Overview*, August 17, 2018, 14. http://edr.state.fl.us/Content/presentations/economic/FlEconomicOverview_8–17–18.pdf. The report states that "by itself, the storm produced a net permanent increase in Florida's population of 53,137 persons."

67. Edwin Meléndez and Jennifer Hinojosa, "Estimates of Post-Hurricane Maria Exodus from Puerto Rico," research brief, Center for Puerto Rican Studies, City University of New York, 2017.

68. Office of Governor Rick Scott, "Governor Rick Scott Issues Updates on State Action to Assist Puerto Ricans," press release, November 29, 2017.

69. Office of Governor Rick Scott, "Gov. Scott Declares State of Emergency for Hurricane Maria to Support Puerto Rico," press release, October 2, 2017.

70. Florida Commissioner of Education Pam Stewart, "Emergency Order Relating to Students and Teachers Displaced by Hurricane Maria" and "Emergency Order Removing Obstacles for Florida College System Institutions Enrolling Students Displaced by Hurricane Maria," October 6, 2017.

71. Florida Legislature Office of Economic and Demographic Research, *Florida: An Economic Overview*, 7, 13.

72. Kate Santich, "Central Florida Affordable Housing: Here's One Big Reason Why There Isn't Enough," *Orlando Sentinel*, October 6, 2018.

73. Kathya Severino, *Post Hurricane Maria: Transitional Shelter Assistance (TSA) and Other Housing Assistance*, Center for Puerto Rican Studies, Policy Brief 2018–01, April 2018, 3, https://centropr.hunter.cuny.edu/sites/default/files/data_briefs/PB2018–01-TSA-APRIL2018_3.pdf.

74. LatinoJustice, "Judge Extends TSA to August 31 Pending Ruling on TRO," press release, August 1, 2018, https://www.latinojustice.org/en/news/judge-extends-tsa-august-31st-pending-ruling-tro. LatinoJustice initially filed a class action suit in the United States District Court for the District of Massachusetts on June 30 seeking a temporary restraining order against FEMA, which was set to end the TSA program on that date. The federal court extended TSA for Hurricane Maria evacuees until July 4 and again until August 31, pending a formal hearing, before ending the TSA program on September 14, 2018. See also LatinoJustice, "Judge Denies Preliminary Injunction for FEMA Aid for Hurricane Maria Evacuees," press release, August 30, 2018, https://www.latinojustice.org/en/news/judge-denies-preliminary-injunction-fema-aid-hurricane-maria-evacuees.

75. Bianca Padró Ocasio, "Housing Aid Extended for Puerto Rico Evacuees, But with Stricter Requirements," *Orlando Sentinel*, March 9, 2018.

76. FEMA News Desk Puerto Rico, email to María Padilla, August 20, 2019.

77. Jennifer A. Marcial Ocasio, "Governor of Puerto Rico Says He Wants Hurricane-Displaced Families to Return to the Island," *Orlando Sentinel,* June 4, 2018.

78. Steven Lemongello, "Central Florida Voter Trends: Bad News for GOP, Mixed Bag for Democrats as Early Voting Kicks Off," *Orlando Sentinel*, August 13, 2018. However, an increasing number of Puerto Ricans and Hispanics are registering with no party affiliation, and these numbers jumped significantly, by 33 percent in Osceola County and 11 percent in Orange County.

79. Bianca Padró Ocasio, "Outreach Group Touted by Puerto Rico Governor a Nonfactor So Far in Florida Voting," *Orlando Sentinel*, August 28, 2018. "We won't have an impact of 100,000 people in three months. That's unrealistic," said one of Poder's board members.

80. LatinoJustice, "Judge Orders Compliance with the Voting Rights Act for Spanish Speaking Voters before 2018 Midterms in Florida," press release, Sep-

tember 7, 2018, https://www.latinojustice.org/en/news/judge-orders-compliance-voting-rights-act-spanish-speaking-voters-2018-midterms-florida. In his ruling, District Court judge Mark E. Walker noted, "It is remarkable that it takes a coalition of voting rights organizations and individuals to sue in federal court to seek minimal compliance with the plain language of a venerable fifty-three-year-old [voting rights] law."

81. Florida News Service, "Federal Judge Asked to Require Spanish-language Ballots in 32 Florida Counties," *Orlando Sentinel*, April 8, 2019.

82. Office of Florida Governor Ron DeSantis, "Governor Ron DeSantis Directs Florida Department of State to Address Availability of Spanish Language Ballots for the 2020 Elections," press release, April 11, 2019.

83. ALG Research, "Florida-Puerto Rican Diaspora Poll," March 12–20, 2019. In the poll, Senator Marco Rubio had total favorability of 40 percent, Puerto Rico governor Ricardo Rosselló 39 percent, and US representative Darren Soto 38 percent.

84. Charles Segal, "Encourage Self Sufficiency," letter to the editor, *Orlando Sentinel,* July 6, 2018. See also José Javier Pérez, "Organizaciones comunitarias evitan que familias queden en las calles de Orlando," *El Nuevo Día*, September 15, 2018, online comments by Víctor García, https://www.elnuevodia.com/corresponsalias/orlando/nota/organizacionescomunitariasevitanquefamiliasquedenenlascalles-deorlando-2447335/.

85. Rosaura Orengo-Aguayo, Regan W. Stewart, et al., "Disaster Exposure and Mental Health among Puerto Rican Youths after Hurricane Maria," *JAMA Network Open*, April 26, 2019, 1, 6. The Puerto Rico Education Department–Medical University of South Carolina survey of 96,108 students was conducted in grades three to twelve across several regions of Puerto Rico and took place five to nine months after Maria. The results are being used to develop trauma-focused resources and programs for schools.

86. Jean Rhodes, Christian Chang, et al., "The Impact of Hurricane Katrina on the Mental and Physical Health of Low-Income Parents in New Orleans," *American Journal of Orthopyschiatry* 80, no. 2 (April 2010): 237–47.

87. Orengo-Aguayo, Stewart, et al., "Disaster Exposure," 2.

88. Danielle Prieur, "UCF Restores Opens a Clinic to Serve the Needs of Displaced Puerto Rican Families," WMFE.org public radio, March 25, 2019.

89. Silver, "Puerto Ricans in Florida," 93.

90. Barbara Gutiérrez, "Battling the Stress of Hurricane Maria," news.miami.edu, January 28, 2019. News story is based on University of Miami Miller School of Medicine study by C. Scaramutti, C. P. Salas-Wright, S. R. Vos, and S. J. Schwartz, "The Mental Health Impact of Hurricane Maria on Puerto Ricans in Puerto Rico and Florida," *Disaster Medicine and Public Health Preparedness* 13, no. 1 (2019): 24–27, doi:10.1017/dmp.2018.151.

91. Héctor R. Cordero-Guzmán and Samantha Vargas, *Opportunity in the Sun-*

shine State: Characteristics of Recent Movers from Puerto Rico to Florida, National
Council of La Raza statistical brief, 2016, 6.

92. Silver, "Puerto Ricans in Florida," 86.

93. Duany, "The Orlando Ricans," 92.

94. *The Tempest*, act 5, scene 1, epilogue, final speech by Prospero, opensource-
shakespeare.org

Chapter 2. Telling Survivors' Stories

1."Upwards of 175,000 People Have Fled Puerto Rico in the Year since Hurricane Maria," press release, Carlos Vargas-Ramos, Center for Puerto Rican
Studies, Hunter College. https://centropr.hunter.cuny.edu/events-news/news/
upwards-175000-people-have-fled-puerto-rico-year-hurricane-maria.

Chapter 3. Living in Hotels

1. Severino, *Post-Hurricane Maria: Transitional Shelter Assistance*, 3. Figure is as
of April 2018.

2. Arnaldo Cruz, "Why Puerto Rico's Fiscal Crisis Could Get Even Worse," *Fiscal Times*, November 20, 2016, http://www.thefiscaltimes.com/2016/11/20/Why-
Puerto-Rico-s-Debt-Crisis-Could-Get-Even-Worse. Toa Baja was in dire financial
straits. In November 2016 the municipality stopped paying its employees after
reporting more than $175 million in long-term debt in 2015 and a negative bank
balance of $14 million. Later, in July 2018, two of Toa Baja's finance staff were
indicted on charges of theft, conversion, and misappropriation of funds from the
US Department of Housing and Urban Development (HUD) and Health and Human Services (HHS) that were used to make payroll and pay contractors. See also
United States Attorney's Office, District of Puerto Rico, "Mayor of the Municipality of Sabana Grande Indicted for Conversion of Federal Funds, Fraud, and Money
Laundering; In a Separate Indictment, Two Ex-Employees of the Municipality of
Toa Baja Indicted and Arrested," press release, July 5, 2018, https://www.justice.
gov/usao-pr/pr/mayor-municipality-sabana-grande-indicted-conversion-federal-
funds-fraud-and-money.

Chapter 4. Settling In

1. Mekela Panditharatne, "FEMA Has Rejected 60 Percent of Assistance Requests in Puerto Rico. Why?" *Slate*, June 15, 2018. FEMA's denial rate for repair
grants in Puerto Rico was reported to be 60 percent, double that of Houston after
Irma, because people couldn't prove ownership of their homes.

2. Frances Robles and Sheri Fink, "Amid Puerto Rico Disaster, Hospital Ship Admitted Just 6 Patients a Day," *New York Times*, December 6, 2017. The US Navy hospital ship *Comfort* was deployed to Puerto Rico but admitted only 290 patients and treated 1,625 people as outpatients during its approximate fifty-three days on the island.

3. Nicole Valdes, "American Cancer Society Organizes Rescue Mission in Puerto Rico," winknews.com, October 25, 2017, http://www.winknews.com/2017/10/25/american-cancer-society-organizes-rescue-mission-in-puerto-rico/. At that point, the American Cancer Society had airlifted about fifty-five cancer patients out of Puerto Rico to the States and had plans to take more. American Cancer Society, "ACS Helps Evacuate Cancer Patients from Puerto Rico," My Society Source, October 18, 2017, mysocietysource.org. The flights were provided by PepsiCo; Johnsonville, a Wisconsin-based sausage company; an anonymous donor from West Palm Beach; and American Cancer Society board member Jorge Luis López.

4. Megan Cerullo, "Pitbull Sends Private Plane to Puerto Rico to Bring Cancer Patients to U.S. Mainland for Chemo," *New York Daily News*, September 26, 2017. Cuban-born rapper Pitbull sent his private plane to rescue cancer patients about one week after the hurricane.

5. Molly Hennessy-Fiske, "In One Puerto Rico Mountain Town, a Wall of Mud Came Crashing Down," *Los Angeles Times*, September 17, 2017. Sisters Irees González Collazo, seventy-four, Carmen González Collazo, seventy-three, and Sara González Collazo, seventy-two, were bedridden and died in their home, buried under a mudslide in the mountain town of Utuado, one of the island's hardest-hit towns.

6. Major League Baseball, "Hurricane Relief Efforts for Puerto Rico," October 2017, mlb.com, https://www.mlb.com/pirates/community/puerto-rico. The Pittsburgh Pirates' players, coach, and front-office staff collected more than 450,000 pounds of supplies for Puerto Rico. In October 9, 2017, the group distributed an estimated seven thousand pounds of goods in Caguas, hometown of Pirates' third-base coach Joey Cora.

7. Associated Press, "Lawmakers Investigate Puerto Rico's Medical Examiner as Bodies Pile Up," cbsnews.com, July 20, 2018, https://www.cbsnews.com/news/puerto-rico-institute-of-forensic-science-investigation/. This news report indicated there were seventy-six bodies in trailers outside of the Institute of Forensic Science in San Juan. An additional 259 bodies were being kept inside the morgue, some dating from 2012. Plus, fifty-six bodies were identified by relatives but remained unclaimed.

Chapter 5. The View from Orlando

1. María T. Padilla, "Hispanics Bloom in Neighborhood," *Orlando Sentinel*, June 13, 1999.

2. Bianca Padró Ocasio, "Puerto Rican Mother's Killing at Kissimmee Motel a Lingering Nightmare, Family Says," *Orlando Sentinel*, May 30, 2018. María "Betzy" Santiago-Burgos was a licensed nurse who fled Puerto Rico after Hurricane Maria and was later shot and killed in May 2018 at a Super 8 motel in Kissimmee by a family friend who had a long-standing obsession with her. She worked at a Dollar Tree store and then a construction job at a Walt Disney World theme park, waiting for her nursing license to be validated in Florida.

3. Robin Respaut and Alvin Báez, "Florida Communities Scramble to Help Displaced Puerto Ricans," *Reuters*, January 12, 2018. Debora Oquendo is a Hurricane Maria survivor who came to the Orlando area with her ten-month-old daughter, initially stayed in a hotel, and was interviewed a number of times by various news organizations during the initial influx of Puerto Rican migrants.

Chapter 6. Conclusion

1. Edwin Meléndez and Jennifer Hinojosa, "Puerto Ricans Keep on Growing! The Puerto Rican Population in the United States Grew at a Rapid Pace between 2016–2017," research brief, Center for Puerto Rican Studies, City University of New York, September 2018.

2. US Census Bureau, Population Division, "Annual Estimates of the Resident Population," April 2019.

3. Meléndez and Hinojosa, "Estimates of Post-Hurricane Maria Exodus from Puerto Rico."

4. Florida Legislature Office of Economic and Demographic Research, *Florida: An Economic Overview*, August 17, 2018, 14.

5. Meléndez and Hinojosa, "Puerto Ricans Keep on Growing!"

6. "Hispanic or Latino Origin by Specific Origin," US Census 2017 American Community Survey, B03001.

7. "Latinos in Central Florida: The Growing Hispanic Presence in the Sunshine State," Hispanic Federation (New York), Summer 2016.

8. Marga Parés Arroyo, "El efecto del huracán María sobre la niñez," *El Nuevo Día*, January 24, 2019. The story cites a study by the Instituto del Desarrollo de la Juventud and Estudios Técnicos that surveyed 705 households with children under the age of eighteen in six municipalities in Puerto Rico.

9. Elizabeth M. Aranda, *Emotional Bridges to Puerto Rico* (Lanham, MD: Rowman and Littlefield, 2007), 42–48: "When we consider the varying routes to incorporation and the impact of the context of reception, we must also consider the resources and opportunities available to Puerto Ricans when they embark on their migration journey."

10. Howard Rodríguez-Mori, "The Information Behavior of Puerto Rican Migrants to Central Florida, 2003–2009: Grounded Analysis of 6 Case Studies Use of

Social Networks during the Migration Process" (Ph.D. diss., Florida State University, 2009).

11. Bianca Padró Ocasio, "Puerto Rican Families Fled Hurricane Maria's Destruction to Panama City: Months Later, Michael Struck," *Orlando Sentinel*, March 29, 2019; "Hurricane Michael Recap: Historic Category 5 Florida Panhandle Landfall and Inland Wind Damage Swath," weather.com, October 13, 2018.

12. Puerto Rico Emergency Management Bureau and Puerto Rico Department of Public Safety, *Joint Operational Catastrophe Incident Plan of Puerto Rico*, June 2019, pdf, p. 3, https://www.scribd.com/document/423665304/Plan-Operacional-Conjunto-para-Incidentes-Catastroficos-de-Puerto-Rico#download&from_embed.

13. "#RickyLeaks" contained 889 pages of texts among the governor and his aides and was published by the Puerto Rico Center for Investigative Journalism, based in San Juan, on July 13, 2019. The full name of the report is *The 889 Pages of the Telegram Chat between Rosselló Nevares and His Closest Aides,* http://periodismoinvestigativo.com/2019/07/the-889-pages-of-the-telegram-chat-between-rossello-nevares-and-his-closest-aides/.

14. Luis J. Valentín Ortiz and Carla Minet, *Las 889 páginas de telegram entre Rosselló Nevares y sus allegados,* Centro de Periodismo Investigativo, July 13, 2019, http://periodismoinvestigativo.com/2019/07/las-889-paginas-de-telegram-entre-rossello-nevares-y-sus-allegados/.

Afterword

1. Johanna López, at "Puerto Rico, Puerto Ricans: In Pursuit of Puerto Rican Studies," research summit in Orlando, University of Central Florida Puerto Rico Research Hub and Center for Puerto Rican Studies, City University of New York, April 17, 2019.

2. Prieur, "UCF Restores Opens a Clinic," WMFE.org public radio, March 25, 2019.

3. Jan Freitag and Claudia Alvarado, "A Look at FEMA Hotel Spending after Harvey and Irma," *hotelnewsnow.com*, June 1, 2018, http://www.hotelnewsnow.com/Articles/286667/A-look-at-FEMA-hotel-spending-after-Irma-and-Harvey.

BIBLIOGRAPHY

ALG Research. "Florida-Puerto Rican Diaspora Poll," 2019.

Andrés, José, and Richard Wolffe. *We Fed an Island*. New York: HarperCollins, 2018.

Aranda, Elizabeth M. *Emotional Bridges to Puerto Rico: Migration, Return Migration, and the Struggles of Incorporation*. Lanham, MD: Rowman and Littlefield, 2018.

Associated Press. "Lawmakers Investigate Puerto Rico's Medical Examiner as Bodies Pile Up." cbsnews.com. July 20, 2018. https://www.cbsnews.com/news/puerto-rico-institute-of-forensic-science-investigation/.

Birson, Kurt. "Puerto Rican Migration and the Brain Drain Dilemma." In *Puerto Ricans at the Dawn of the New Millennium*, edited by Edwin Meléndez and Carlos Vargas-Ramos. New York: Center for Puerto Rican Studies, City University of New York, 2014.

Bravin, Jess. "Supreme Court Strikes down Puerto Rico Debt-Restructuring Law." *Wall Street Journal*, June 13, 2016.

Cerullo, Megan. "Pitbull Sends Private Plane to Puerto Rico to Bring Cancer Patients to U.S. Mainland for Chemo." *New York Daily News*, September 26, 2017.

Comité Multisectorial para el Reto Demográfico. *Resumen del informe de progreso: Acercamiento a problemas y soluciones*. San Juan: Government of Puerto Rico, 2018.

Cordero-Guzmán, Hector R., and Samantha Vargas. *Opportunity in the Sunshine State: Characteristics of Recent Movers from Puerto Rico to Florida*. Washington, DC: National Council of La Raza, 2016.

Corkery, Michael, and Mary Williams Walsh. "Puerto Rico's Governor Says Island's Debt Is 'Not Payable.'" *New York Times*, June 28, 2015.

Cruz, Arnaldo. "Why Puerto Rico's Fiscal Crisis Could Get Even Worse." *Fiscal Times*, November 20, 2016. http://www.thefiscaltimes.com/2016/11/20/Why-Puerto-Rico-s-Debt-Crisis-Could-Get-Even-Worse.

Denis, Nelson A. *War Against All Puerto Ricans*. New York: Nation Books, 2015.

Duany, Jorge. "The Orlando Ricans: Overlapping Identity Discourses among Middle-Class Puerto Rican Immigrants." *CENTRO: Journal of the Center for Puerto Rican Studies* 22, no. 1 (Spring 2010): 85–115.

———. *The Puerto Rican Nation on the Move, Identities on the Island and in the United States*. Chapel Hill: University of North Carolina Press, 2002.

Federal Emergency Management Agency (FEMA). *2017 Hurricane Season FEMA After-Action Report*. 2018. https://www.fema.gov/media-library/assets/documents/167249.

———. *Resources Are Available to Survivors as FEMA's Transitional Sheltering Assistance Program Ends*. HQ-18-0-FactSheet, 2018.

Flores, Juan. *Essays on Puerto Rican Identity*. Houston: Arte Público, 1993.

Florida Legislature Office of Economic and Demographic Research. *Florida: An Economic Overview*. 2018. http://edr.state.fl.us/Content/presentations/economic/FlEconomicOverview_8-17-18.pdf.

Freitag, Jan, and Claudia Alvarado. "A Look at FEMA Hotel Spending after Harvey and Irma." *hotelnewsnow.com*. June 1, 2018. http://www.hotelnewsnow.com/Articles/286667/A-look-at-FEMA-hotel-spending-after-Irma-and-Harvey.

García, José Manuel. *Voices from Mariel: Oral Histories of the 1980 Cuban Boatlift*. Gainesville: University Press of Florida, 2018.

George Washington University, Milken Institute of Public Health. *Ascertainment of the Estimated Excess Mortality from Hurricane Maria in Puerto Rico*. 2018. https://publichealth.gwu.edu/sites/default/files/downloads/projects/PRstudy/Acertainment%20of%20the%20Estimated%20Excess%20Mortality%20from%20Hurricane%20Maria%20in%20Puerto%20Rico.pdf.

González, José Luis. *The Four-Storeyed Country*. Maplewood, NJ: Waterfront, 1990.

Government Accounting Office (GAO). *2017 Hurricanes and Wildfires, Initial Observations on the Federal Response and Key Recovery Challenges*. 2018.

Government of Puerto Rico. *Transformation and Innovation in the Wake of Devastation: An Economic and Disaster Recovery Plan for Puerto Rico: Report to Congress*. 2018. http://www.p3.pr.gov/assets/pr-transformation-innovation-plan-congressional-submission-080818.pdf.

Gutiérrez, Barbara. "Battling the Stress of Hurricane Maria." news.miami.edu. January 28, 2019. https://news.miami.edu/stories/2019/01/hurricane-maria-survivors-in-central-and-south-florida-experienced-higher-mental-stress.html.

Gutiérrez, John A. "Latinos in Central Florida: The Growing Hispanic Presence in the Sunshine State." Hispanic Federation, 2016.

Hennessy-Fiske, Molly. "In One Puerto Rico Mountain Town, a Wall of Mud Came Crashing Down." *Los Angeles Times*, September 17, 2017.

History Task Force, Center for Puerto Rican Studies. *Labor Migration under Capitalism: The Puerto Rican Experience*. New York: City University of New York, 1979.

Houser, Trevor, and Peter Marsters. *The World's Second Largest Blackout*. Report. RHG.com. April 12, 2018. https://rhg.com/research/puerto-rico-hurricane-maria-worlds-second-largest-blackout/.

"Hurricanes: Science and Society." University of Rhode Island. hurricane-science. org. https://www.hurricanescience.org/history/storms/1920s/.

Hurston, Zora Neale. *Their Eyes Were Watching God*. Chicago: University of Illinois Press, 1978.

Karni, Annie, and Patricia Mazzei. "Trump Lashes Out Again at Puerto Rico, Bewildering the Island." *New York Times*, April 2, 2019.

Kishore, Nishant, Domingo Marqués, Ayesha Mahmud, et al. "Mortality in Puerto Rico after Hurricane Maria." *New England Journal of Medicine*. Special Report 379. May 2018, 162–70. https://www.nejm.org/doi/full/10.1056/NEJMsa1803972.

LatinoJustice. "Judge Extends TSA to August 31 Pending Ruling on TRO." Press release, 2018. https://www.latinojustice.org/en/news/judge-extends-tsa-august-31st-pending-ruling-tro.

———. "Judge Orders Compliance with the Voting Rights Act for Spanish Speaking Voters before 2018 Midterms in Florida." Press release, 2018. https://www.latinojustice.org/en/news/judge-orders-compliance-voting-rights-act-spanish-speaking-voters-2018-midterms-florida.

Lemongello, Steven. "Central Florida Voter Trends: Bad News for GOP, Mixed Bag for Democrats as Early Voting Kicks Off." *Orlando Sentinel*, August 13, 2018.

Major League Baseball. "Hurricane Relief Efforts for Puerto Rico." mlb.com. October 2017. https://www.mlb.com/pirates/community/puerto-rico.

Marcial Ocasio, Jennifer A. "Governor of Puerto Rico Says He Wants Hurricane-Displaced Families to Return to the Island." *Orlando Sentinel*, June 4, 2018.

Meléndez, Edwin. "Upwards of 175,000 People Have Fled Puerto Rico in the Year since Hurricane Maria." Press release by Carlos Vargas-Ramos. Center for Puerto Rican Studies, City University of New York, 2018.

———. "U.S. Citizenship in Puerto Rico: One Hundred Years after the Jones Act." *CENTRO: Journal of the Center for Puerto Rican Studies* 29, no. 1, 2017.

Meléndez, Edwin, and Jennifer Hinojosa. "Estimates of Post-Hurricane Maria Exodus from Puerto Rico." Research brief. Center for Puerto Rican Studies, City University of New York, 2017.

———. "Puerto Ricans Keep on Growing! The Puerto Rican Population in the United States Grew at a Rapid Pace between 2016–2017." Research brief. Center for Puerto Rican Studies, City University of New York, 2018.

Meléndez, Edwin, and Edgardo Meléndez, eds. *Colonial Dilemma, Critical Perspectives on Contemporary Puerto Rico*. Boston: South End Press, 1993.

Meléndez, Edwin, and Carlos Vargas-Ramos, eds. *Puerto Ricans at the Dawn of the New Millennium*. New York: Center for Puerto Rican Studies, City University of New York, 2014.

"The Mind-bending and Heart-breaking Economics of Hurricane Maria." Climate Impact Lab. ImpactLab.org. http://www.impactlab.org/news-insights/the-mind-bending-and-heart-breaking-economics-of-hurricane-maria/.

Monge, José Trías. *Puerto Rico: The Trials of the Oldest Colony in the World.* New Haven: Yale University Press, 2017.

Morales Carrión, Arturo. *Puerto Rico, a Political and Cultural History.* New York: Norton, 1983.

Nakamura, David. "'It Totally Belittled the Moment': Many Look Back in Dismay at Trump's Tossing of Paper Towels in Puerto Rico." *Washington Post*, September 13, 2018.

Neuman, Gerald L., and Tomiko Brown-Nagrin, eds. *Reconsidering the Insular Cases: The Past and Future of the American Empire.* Boston: Harvard Law School Human Rights Program, Signature Book Printing, 2015.

Office of Florida Governor Rick Scott. "Gov. Scott Declares State of Emergency for Hurricane Maria to Support Puerto Rico." Press release. 2017.

———. "Governor Rick Scott Issues Updates on State Action to Assist Puerto Ricans." Press release. 2017.

Office of Florida Governor Ron DeSantis. "Governor Ron DeSantis Directs Florida Department of State to Address Availability of Spanish Language Ballots for the 2020 Elections." Press release. 2019.

Ojito, Mirta. *Finding Mañana: A Memoir of a Cuban Exodus.* New York: Penguin, 2005.

Orengo-Aguayo, Rosaura, Regan W. Stewart, et al. "Disaster Exposure and Mental Health among Puerto Rican Youths after Hurricane María." *JAMA Network Open.* 2019; 2(4):e192619, 2019.

Padilla, María T. "Hispanics Bloom in Neighborhood." *Orlando Sentinel.* June 13, 1999. https://www.orlandosentinel.com/news/os-xpm-1999-06-13-9906130099-story.html.

———. "Hurricane Maria Galvanizes Puerto Ricans in Central Florida." orlandolatino.org (blog). September 22, 2017. http://orlandolatino.org/2017/09/hurricane-maria/.

———. "The Push for Puerto Rico Statehood." *orlandolatino.org* (blog). March 29, 2019. http://orlandolatino.org/2019/03/puerto-rico-statehood/.

Padró Ocasio, Bianca. "Housing Aid Extended for Puerto Rico Evacuees, But with Stricter Requirements." *Orlando Sentinel*, March 9, 2018.

———. "Outreach Group Touted by Puerto Rico Governor a Nonfactor So Far in Florida Voting." *Orlando Sentinel*, August 28, 2018.

———. "Puerto Rican Families Fled Hurricane Maria's Destruction to Panama City. Months Later, Michael Struck." *Orlando Sentinel*, March 29, 2019.

———. "Puerto Rican Mother's Killing at Kissimmee Motel a Lingering Nightmare, Family Says." *Orlando Sentinel*, May 30, 2018.

Panditharatne, Makela. "FEMA Has Rejected 60 Percent of Assistance Requests in Puerto Rico. Why?" *Slate*, June 15, 2018.

Parés-Arroyo, Marga. "El efecto del huracán María sobre la niñez." *El Nuevo Día*, January 24, 2019. https://www.elnuevodia.com/noticias/locales/nota/elefectodelhuracanmariasobrelaninez-2472768/.

Puerto Rico Emergency Management Bureau and Puerto Rico Department of Public Safety. *Joint Operational Catastrophe Incident Plan of Puerto Rico*. June 2019. pdf. https://www.scribd.com/document/423665304/Plan-Operacional-Conjunto-para-Incidentes-Catastroficos-de-Puerto-Rico#download&from_embed.

Puerto Rico Planning Board. "Table 1: Selected Series of Income and Product, Total and Per capita." *Statistical Appendix of the Economic Report to the Governor and to the Legislative Assembly*. 2017.

Respaut, Robin, and Alvin Báez. "Florida Communities Scramble to Help Displaced Puerto Ricans." *Reuters*, January 12, 2018.

Rhodes, Jean, Christian Chang, et al. "The Impact of Hurricane Katrina on the Mental and Physical Health of Low-Income Parents in New Orleans." *American Journal of Orthopsychiatry* 80, no. 2 (April 2010): 237–47.

Robles, Frances. "Puerto Rico Spent 11 Months Turning the Power Back On: They Finally Got to Her." *New York Times*, August 14, 2018.

Robles, Frances, and Sheri Fink. "Amid Puerto Rico Disaster, Hospital Ship Admitted Just 6 Patients a Day." *New York Times*, December 6, 2017.

Rodríguez, José, and Deborah Beidel. "UCF Restores Opens a Clinic to Serve the Needs of Displaced Puerto Rican Families." Interview by Danielle Prieur. Central Florida News, *WMFE*. March 25, 2019. https://www.wmfe.org/ucf-restores-opens-a-clinic-to-serve-the-needs-of-displaced-puerto-rican-families/99425.

Rodríguez, Richard. *Hunger of Memory*. New York: Bantam, 1983.

Rodríguez-Mori, Howard. "The Information Behavior of Puerto Rican Migrants to Central Florida, 2003–2009: Grounded Analysis of 6 Case Studies Use of Social Networks during the Migration Process." Ph.D. diss., Florida State University, 2009.

Santiago, Esmeralda. *When I Was Puerto Rican*. New York: Vintage, 1993.

Santich, Kate. "Central Florida Affordable Housing: Here's One Big Reason Why There Isn't Enough." *Orlando Sentinel*, October 6, 2018.

Schwartz, Stuart B. "The Hurricane of San Ciriaco: Disaster, Politics, and Society in Puerto Rico, 1899–1901. *Hispanic American Historical Review* 72, no. 3 (August 1991).

———. "Puerto Rico's Hurricane Maria Proves Once Again That Natural Disasters Are Never Natural." *historynewsnetork.org*, October 2, 2017. https://historynewsnetwork.org/article/167090.

Severino, Kathya. *Post Hurricane María: Transitional Shelter Assistance (TSA) and Other Housing Assistance*. Center for Puerto Rican Studies. Policy brief, 2018.

https://centropr.hunter.cuny.edu/sites/default/files/data_briefs/PB2018–01-TSA-APRIL2018_3.pdf.

Shakespeare, William. *The Tempest*. http://www.opensourceshake.org/views/play/plays_view.php?WorkID=tempest&Act=5&Scene=1&Scope=scene.

Silver, Patricia. "Puerto Ricans in Florida." In *Puerto Ricans in the New Millennium*, edited by Edwin Meléndez and Carlos Vargas Ramos. New York: Center for Puerto Rican Studies, 2014.

Sosa, Omayra. "Se disparan en casi mil las muertes tras Maria." periodismoinvestigativo.com, 2017. http://periodismoinvestigativo.com/2017/12/se-disparan-en-casi-mil-las-muertes-tras-maria/.

Sotomayor, Sonia. *My Beloved Island*. New York: Vintage, 2014.

Sparrow, Bartholomew H. *The Insular Cases and the Emergence of American Empire*. Lawrence: University Press of Kansas, 2006.

Stargardter, Gabriel, and Dave Graham. "Trump Lays Blame on Puerto Ricans for Slow Hurricane Response." *Reuters*, September 30, 2017.

Stewart, Pam. "Emergency Order Relating to Students and Teachers Displaced by Hurricane Maria." Florida Department of Education. 2017. http://www.fldoe.org/core/fileparse.php/5673/urlt/FinalOrderK1210617.pdf.

———. "Emergency Order Removing Obstacles for Florida College System Institutions Enrolling Students Displaced by Hurricane Maria." Florida Department of Education. 2017. http://www.fldoe.org/core/fileparse.php/5673/urlt/FinalOrderFCS10617.pdf.

Sullivan, Eileen, Julie Hirschfeld Davis, and Nicholas Fandos. "Trump Denies Puerto Rico Death Toll, Falsely Accusing Democrats of Inflating the Numbers." *New York Times*, September 13, 2018.

Torruela, Juan R. "The Insular Cases. A Declaration of Their Bankruptcy and My Harvard Pronouncement." In *Reconsidering the Insular Cases, the Past and Future of the American Empire*, edited by Gerald L. Neuman, 61–76. Boston: Harvard Law School Human Rights Program, 2015.

———. "The Insular Cases: The Establishment of a Regime of Political Apartheid." 29 U. Pa. J. Int'l L. 283 (2007).

United States Congress. *Congressional Task Force on Economic Growth in Puerto Rico: Report to the House and Senate*. Congressional Report, 2016.

Valentín Ortiz, Luis J., and Carla Minet. *The 889 Pages of the Telegram Chat between Rosselló Nevares and His Closest Aides*. Puerto Rico Center for Investigative Journalism. http://periodismoinvestigativo.com/2019/07/the-889-pages-of-the-telegram-chat-between-rossello-nevares-and-his-closest-aides/.

Venator-Santiago, Charles. "Today, Being Born in Puerto Rico Is Tantamount to Being Born in the United States." In "U.S. Citizenship in Puerto Rico: One Hundred Years after the Jones Act." *CENTRO: Journal of the Center for Puerto Rican Studies* 29, no. 1 (2017).

Walsh, Mary Williams. "Puerto Rico Declares a Form of Bankruptcy." *New York Times*, May 3, 2017.

Willison, C. E., P. M. Singer, M. S. Creary, et al. "Quantifying Inequities in U.S. Federal Response to Hurricane Disaster in Texas and Florida Compared with Puerto Rico." *BMJ Global Health*, 2019. https://gh.bmj.com/content/4/1/e001191.

Zezima, Katie. "Puerto Rico Pushes for Statehood, Calling It a Civil Rights Issue." *Washington Post*, June 27, 2018.

INDEX

Page numbers in *italics* refer to photographs.

MARÍA T. PADILLA is a journalist based in Orlando, Florida, with more than thirty-five years of experience in newspaper reporting, including with five daily newspapers and two Spanish-language weeklies. She is the editor and founder of OrlandoLatino.org, a blog that voices issues important to Orlando's Latino community.

NANCY ROSADO is a retired NYPD sergeant with more than thirty-five years of combined professional experience in mental health, law enforcement, community engagement, and disaster response. A graduate of Fordham University's Graduate School of Social Work, she is currently a consultant and the outreach coordinator for the Puerto Rican, LGBTQ, and law enforcement communities at the University of Central Florida's RESTORES trauma treatment program.